26

a b c d e f g h i j k l m n o p q r s t u v w x y z

A journal of poetry and poetics

SAN FRANCISCO BAY AREA ° 2004

Editors: Avery E. D. Burns, Rusty Morrison, Joseph Noble,
Elizabeth Robinson, Brian Strang
Intern: Kay Elliott

Cover design and logo: Jacek Ostoya
Interior design and typesetting: Jaime Robles

ISBN 1-889098-05-1

Web Address: www.26magazine.com

Send submissions to **26**, P.O. Box 4450, Saint Mary's College, Moraga, CA 94575-4730. We read submissions from April 15–July 15. Notification occurs in September. All submissions should be accompanied by a SASE. We do not accept electronic submissions at this time.

Subscriptions: $20 per year; tax deductible lifetime subscription $260. All additional contributions are deeply appreciated and tax deductible. $12 individual issues.

Copyright 2004 by **26**. All rights revert to authors upon publication.

Distributed by Small Press Distribution, Berkeley, CA. (510) 524-1668. email: orders@spdbooks.org

Indexed by *The American Humanities Index*.

We, the editors of **26**, would like to thank the William and Flora Hewlett Foundation for their support of this issue. We thank the University of California at Santa Cruz for permission to print the work of Kenneth Patchen on our cover and endsheet.

SAINT MARY'S COLLEGE
of California

26 is affiliated with the Saint Mary's College MFA Program in Creative Writing. For more information about the program contact Christopher Sindt at 925-631-4088.

Contents

	ix	EDITORIAL STATEMENT
Paul Celan	1	*from* LIGHTDURESS
translated from German by Pierre Joris		
Martine Bellen	14	LIVING WITH ANIMALS
Drew Kunz	18	*from* NEARBY SO MUCH REMAINS
Jane Wolff	21	*from* DELTA PRIMER
Monica Regan	31	*from* MEASURED IN CIRCLES
Loren Chasse	37	SITE SONOLOGIES #1 & 2
Albert Flynn DeSilver	41	FOR MAXIMUS
Edric Mesmer	42	ARENDT'S LAW
	43	OLIVE LULLABY
Linda Norton	44	THE FEN
Laura Sims	45	DEMOCRACY
	46	SUFFERING SUCCOTASH
Eric Selland	47	*from* TABLE OF PRIMARIES
Loren Chasse	49	SITE SONOLOGY #3
Erica Bernheim	51	PAVESE SAID DEATH WILL COME BEARING YOUR EYES
kari edwards	53	A TRUMPETING THEME SONG
	55	APPLICATIONS WILL BE ACKNOWLEDGED
David Harrison Horton	56	*from* BEI HAI: NORTH OF THE SEA
Andrew Felsinger	61	HYSTERICAL MATERIALISM
Jen Scappettone	62	...FROM THE TIME OF THE ROYAL TOMBS OF UR
Mark Wallace	64	*from* BELIEF IS IMPOSSIBLE
Loren Chasse	66	SITE SONOLOGY #4
Anthony Hawley	68	ICEFIELD SONNETS
Elizabeth Willis	71	ENCHANTER'S NIGHTSHADE
	72	FEMALE FIGS SUPPOSED TO BE MONSTERS

	73	METEORIC FLOWERS
Edwin Torres	74	THE MYTH OF A POPULAR DISTANCE
Brandon Downing	80	CXXIX *from* LAKE ANTIQUITY
Laura Walker	81	SIX PORTRAITS OF THE LETTER B
Trina Baker	84	THE PILGRIM STUMBLES
Ben Lerner	85	*from* THE LICTHENBERG FIGURES
Loren Chasse	87	SITE SONOLOGY #5
Linda Norton	89	MINE
Jack Collum	90	FIRST SIP OF WINE
Dana Teen Lomax	98	*from* NOTE
Laynie Browne	99	*from* FESTOON DICTIONARY
Sarah Mangold	103	HOMESICK IN PARENTHESIS
	105	OK ANTARTICA
Rod Smith	106	HOMAGE TO HOMAGE TO CREELEY
Linda Norton	111	HESITATION KIT
	112	AT A SUPPER CLUB
Christine Moore	113	GEOGRAPHIES OF SEVEN
Joshua Edwards	116	*from* SAG HARBOR
Lisa Samuels	118	PROGRESS
Lisa Lubasch	119	[THE INCREMENT BEGINS]
Andrew Joron	121	THE SOLID OF SOUND
Brian Lucas	125	AN IMPERFECT SHAPE
	126	MUSEUM OF EVERYDAY
Denise Newman and Stephen Whitney	127	NOTES TO THE ARCHITECT
Loren Chasse	130	SITE SONOLOGY #6
Kerri Sonnenberg	133	*from* WAKE
Orlando White	138	OPEN DARK
	140	LOWER CASE i AND j
	142	IMAGES OF MYSELF

	144	Fill in the blank
	146	Blank circle
	148	The i is a cricket
James Meetze	150	*from* Instrument
Julia Bloch	157	*from* The Continuous Present
Dennis Phillips	159	*from* Studies for the Possibility of Hope
Karl Gartung	162	Photos of Lorine Neidecker's Home

Essays & Reviews

Christopher Sindt	169	A Gentler Scion to the Wildest Stock: Some Notes on Contemporary Eco-poetics
Marcella Durand	181	The Ecology of Poetry
Seth Nehil	191	Regarding mutually embedded environments
Steve Roden	195	resonant cities— complete notes:
Loren Chasse	200	an ear afoot
Mark Wallace	206	Looking Beyond the Fields of Poetry
Dale Smith	212	In Time: Joanne Kyger and the Narrative of Every Day
Kristen Hanlon	225	Elizabeth Willis: *Turneresque*
Brian Teare	227	Baptista, Josely Vianna: *On the Shining Screen of the Eyelids.*
Craig Morgan Teicher	235	John Isles: *Ark*
Contributors	240	

26

In "Wilderness," Lorine Niedecker writes, "You are my other country/and I find it hard going." Other images in her poem are of a prickly pear, a violent storm, and "the torrent to raise the river/to float the wounded doe." Niedecker was indisputably a poet of her own environment, and her poems record the struggle to survive and shape the rigors life threw her way. Her work is suffused with place, with the press of season and circumstance, with the peculiar music and imagery of her local experience. At the same time, she claimed a larger environment, traveling time to converse with, say, Michelangelo or Thomas Jefferson. She strolls the South Lawn with J.F.K. after the Bay of Pigs equally as she explores the Galapagos with Darwin. Niedecker understood, as does Joanne Kyger (whose work is discussed in this issue of **26**) that time, too, is an environment. It's malleable narrative can become a "lens through which, slowly, experience of the world is sharpened." Even so, this grappling with environment is hard going. Experience is not necessarily congenial, though it can afford us a clarified sense of possibility: possibility may rise to attention as limitation. Niedecker's work exemplifies this well. The constraints of economics, geography, and imagination shaped a distinctive poetry. Niedecker's work foresees what Marcella Durand says in another of the essays in this issue, that a sustainable ecopoetics attends to the confluence of matter with perception, and something obsolete is therefore recycled into something else.

By now, it can perhaps go without saying that this issue of **26** is oriented around the theme of "environment." The editors chose this particular focus because we felt that it provided a helpful plasticity that enables the discussion of the magazine to embrace diverse understandings. Consider this dictionary definition of "environment:" "the aggregate of surrounding things, conditions or influence, especially as affecting the existence or development of someone or something." Our hope is that we can begin to represent our sense that this aggregate is multi-vocal, contradictory, untidy—a product of ecological harmonies and dissonances. Elements of this aggregate might provide an animating friction, as Seth Nehil notes in "Regarding Mutually Embedded Environments," in which "elements coexist as symbiotic context for their difference." Issue C of **26** has thus brought together an array of texts and images, many of these notations of environment. The poems included here seemed to us to explore a similar range of intent without necessarily being "environment" poems. Notably, we have included more images than in our previous two issues. We have also a generous sampling of work from three musicians/sound artists whose attunement to, and interactions with, auditory material offer another iteration of environment as both site and agent.

Garret Hardin's seminal 1968 article "The Tragedy of the Commons" calls us humans to the hard fact of this planet's finitude. Hardin argues that commonly held land and resources cannot be subdivided infinitely. Those resources become degraded or simply disappear. In order to reassess the common good, it is necessary that—for human participants within the balance of the environment—the optimum become less than the maximum. And how does this pertain to poetry and poetics? In his discussion in "A Gentler Scion to the Wildest Stock," Christopher Sindt suggests that "[t]o some extent ecological poetry must be seen as relational, a linguistic means by which poets come to terms with human responses to natural systems." Human attention does have a useful role to play in this grappling. We as poets need not romanticize nature, nor should we valorize the role of human agency over nature, but neither can we disacknowledge that humans are a part of the given environment and that their attentions could potentially have some restorative efficacy. Artist Jane Wolff observes that the "landscapes we inhabit exist not only as physical realities but also as ideas, and the ways in which we imagine, describe, and represent them have a powerful impact on our plans for their future." Exerting attention may be a means by which humans come to understand their limitations and develop some humility in relation to the nature that surrounds and infuses them. Mark Wallace states this similarly in "Looking Beyond the Fields of Poetry" when he asserts that poetry is not merely a field of discrete objects, but an "exploration of how language permeates the world. . .of the other ways that language *could* permeate the world."

In closing, we thank the University of California at Santa Cruz for permitting us to reproduce one of Kenneth Patchen's poem-paintings on our cover. Patchen's prescient, admonitory work engages with both the beauty and the pain of life in a fragile environment. Like Niedecker, Patchen's work acknowleges the process as hard going, but admonishes us that there is still an optimum to be sought and experienced.

Paul Celan   Translated from German by Pierre Joris

12 *Poems from* Cycle II of
LIGHTDURESS

>Once, death was much in demand,
>   you hid in me.

HATCHETSWARMS
above us,

conversations
with socket-axes in the lowland —

islandpasture, you,
with hope
fogging you
in.

Precognition bleeds
twice behind the curtain,

Cognizance
pearls

TWO AT BRANCUSI'S

If one among these stones
were to tell
what silences it:
here, nearby,
on this old man's crutch-stick,
it would open, as a wound,
into which you'd have to dive,
lonely,
far from my scream, the already also
hewn, white one.

WHERE I forgot myself in you,
you became thought,

something
rushes through us both:
the first of the
world's last
wings,

the hide
overgrows
my storm-riddled
mouth,

you
come not
to
you.

LONG AGO boarded mudskiff.

A but-
ton, come
off,
nitpicks every buttercup,

the hour, the toad,
unhinges its world.

If I gulped down the cartrut,
I'd be with it too.

TODTNAUBERG

Arnica, eyebright, the
draft from the well with the
star-die on top,

in the
Hütte,

written in the book
—whose name did it record
before mine—?
in this book
the line about
a hope, today,
for a thinker's
word
to come,
in the heart,

forest sward, unleveled,
orchis and orchis, singly,

crudeness, later, while driving,
clearly,

he who drives us, the man,
he who also hears it,

the half-
trod log-
trails on the highmoor,
humidity,
much.

SINK away from
the crook of my arm,

take the One
pulse beat along,

hide yourself in it,
outside.

Now, that the prayerstools burn,
I eat the book
with all the
insignia.

TO A BROTHER IN ASIA

The self-transfigured
cannons
drive toward heaven,

ten
bombers yawn,

a running fire blooms,
as surely as peace,

a handful of rice
expires as your friend.

JOSTLED along the delusion-run
by someone who read:
Scab and scurf. Scurf and scab.

To vault the sleep-buck, o once.

How YOU die out in me:

even in the last
threadbare
breath-knot
you stick with one
splinter
life.

Martine Bellen

Living with Animals

Her room lit by the cache of a thousand creatures
                            Their thorny hooded habits

                With shrew-nets, dream-rods,
She catches her keep.

                                o

            Nocturnal spirits play secretive, rarely seen, most at home
                                    On ground but climb trees
Or hyphenate wing and air — soaring through the transparent prison,
                Partaking in oral transportation,
                    Moving through sound and speech.

                                o

    None lightened without adding lightness
                Flavor for euphony
  Like cheesecake batter in a yellowware bowl
              Craft the body spiritual and it will glow
        A moon spoon for mixing words
How co-life aspires
Headlamps hold night-frogs. Dixie Cups, polliwogs.

                  o

Falling from the sky and floating, a melody
    Leaves
        Its unfinished line
                In memory

        The soul's sphericity. Through marbleized
        Eyes. Tambourines.
            Cat's harlequin carnival.

                  o

A round-up of abstracted Arabians
                                        Hazy paint drays
                      Quicken / drear
Variation of song and sense
                          In one fugue state or another
This fairy ring of yearlings trailing an areola along nerves
                                            Of insect's iridescent wing.

o

    Aristophanes, Hitchcock
        Draw light on imaginings
            Hawk & owl descend during new moon
          Unlike cumulus cloud pets, the dispossessed
X ray through darkness
        Break an oath that binds bird to bird.

    A constellation of warblers undulate in sealed captivity
By her bedside
        Rests a jar of black glass
            She breathes the breath of flight
    Cardinal points.

o

Once upon a time, they shed
    Their scales.
             Tumbling into reverie.
Pressure on night's reduced darkness
          Or failure to adhere
To demands of the waking dead: Their double, amphibious lives
    Perpetually encircling a soul describing escape:
                      The haunt.

Drew Kunz

from Nearby so much remains

A dark fabric unravels itself in the mirror. Not a doorway but a companion or sometimes enemy. Standing by the window as the morning moves in and out of. Walls throb, juniper burns, an opaque breath.

o

So what are you to make of it? Thalassic memory. Naked along the columns and squares so saturated with heat. However, just inches from the shadow. Oblate.

o

Stare at a couple suddenly
paused to listen. Susurration.
Palms. Thread of tiny skulls
strung together, release,
wrap around the wrist.

o

This is the tree honored by
Arabs and Greeks alike. Limbs
bent over the low wall, ghosts
float over her lips. "Bruised flesh
on a diseased bone is bad."

o

Or else at the table where a map
collapses and a sentence trails
off. Taramasalata, a small
Polaroid, this island between
two blue points surrounded by
transudatory leaves. As kids
bicycle past.

o

You race through the gates of
the old spa, or what used to be.
A white bird turns bluish, then
black, then dissolves. History,
built on conjecture and ob-
servation, stone and postcards.

o

A walk along the slabs-
pronounce the sun. Sometimes
she sits in the ruins encircled by
weeds. Withdrawn from the
clutter of houses that slip into
the street. Rest in the margin of
an abandoned slope.

o

Nearby so much remains. To
move away brings you closer.
You. Always in the plural, always
unfolding in a multiplication of
persistent dreams.

Jane Wolff

from Delta Primer

The landscapes we inhabit exist not only as physical realities but also as ideas, and the ways in which we imagine, describe, and represent them have a powerful impact on our plans for their future.

The way people see landscapes is especially important in places like the California Delta, where there is enormous pressure for change and fierce debate about what form it should take. The Delta is a hybrid landscape: its strange geography is the result of unpredictable interactions between natural process and cultural intervention; it plays a central role in California's economy and ecology; and its continued existence demands intense human management.

One of the greatest threats to the Delta is its invisibility. Although it is the largest tidal estuary on the West Coast and the centerpiece of the system that supplies water to Southern California, few people know about it, and even fewer can understand the technical terms in which it is usually discussed.

Delta Primer is designed to raise grassroots consciousness about the Delta and its essential part in the lives of all Californians. It describes the landscape in terms of four ideas: that it is a garden, a machine, a wilderness, and a toy. Each of those ideas is illustrated by drawings of artifacts, practices, and processes that comprise the landscape, and all together the drawings make up a standard deck of playing cards. Any game in which the deck is used can become a discussion about the particular circumstances of the Delta, their relative values, and their possible tradeoffs. The goal of the project is to put information quite literally into the hands of the people who depend on this remarkable place and who will, sooner or later, be asked to vote on its future.

2

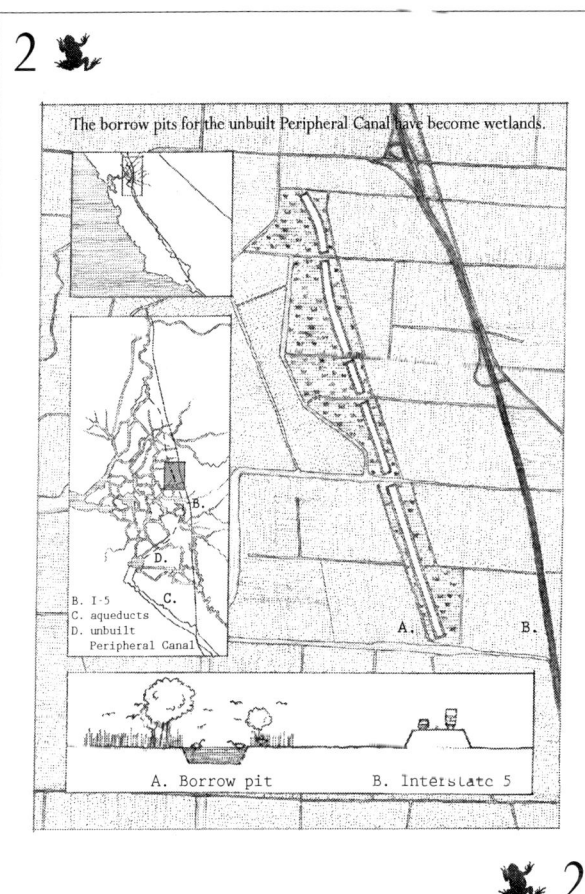

The borrow pits that follow Highway 5 along the edge of the Delta were supposed to have been part of the Peripheral Canal. The canal was never finished, though, and the abandoned trenches became habitat for wetland plants and animals.

Conceived as a machine, the borrow pits have become a wilderness

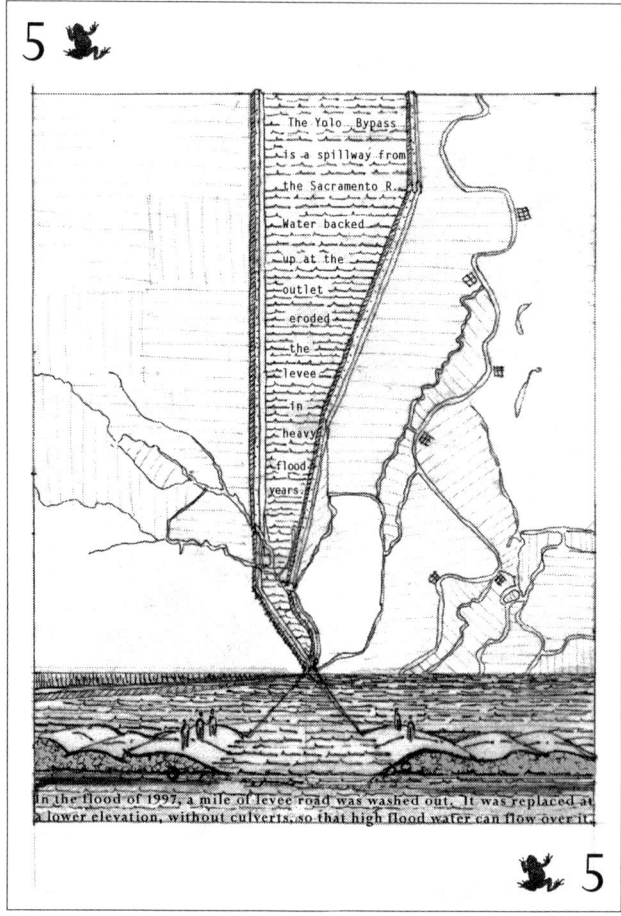

In 1997 the Cache Slough levee buckled and crumpled under the force of the water at the bottleneck. What the flood left behind looked like earthquake damage.

The bypass circumvents the problem of flooding in Sacramento, but it does not diminish the violence of the water. Moving the flood is not the same as controlling it.

3 🍐

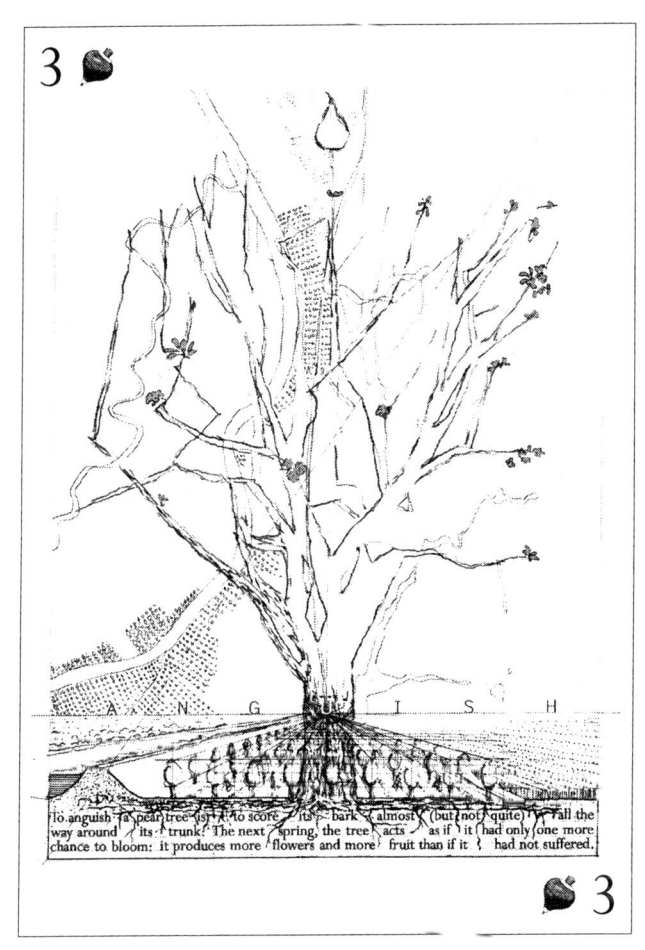

"Shade trees don't make fruit."

When asked why he raises different kinds of pears, Malcolm McCormack, a grower in the north Delta, said, "To play."

A N G U I S H

To anguish a pear tree is to score its bark almost (but not quite) all the way around its trunk. The next spring, the tree acts as if it had only one more chance to bloom: it produces more flowers and more fruit than if it had not suffered.

🍐 3

What is the relationship between a farmer and the plants he cultivates? Does a pear tree have a soul? What does the metaphor of anguishing describe? Is it the tree that suffers, or the farmer?

4

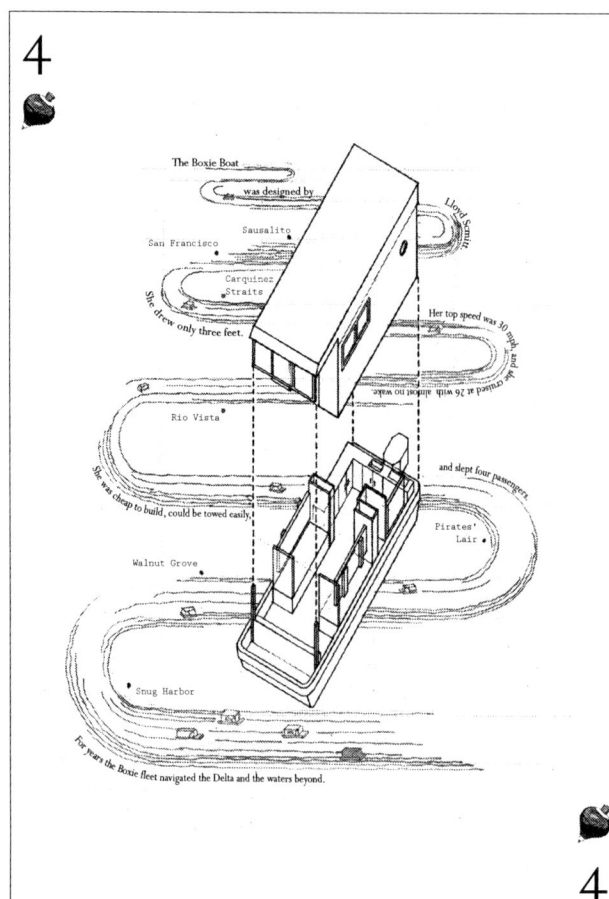

The Boxie Boat was designed by Lloyd Smith.
San Francisco
Sausalito
Carquinez Straits
She drew only three feet.
Her top speed was 30 mph, and she cruised at 26 with almost no wake.
Rio Vista
and slept four passengers
She was cheap to build, could be towed easily,
Pirates' Lair
Walnut Grove
Snug Harbor
For years the Boxie fleet navigated the Delta and the waters beyond.

Made of off-the-shelf parts and easy to pilot, the Boxie Boat was a houseboat for Everyman.

A wide range of people bought Boxie Boats. They formed a Boxie Club, and they cruised together around the Delta and out to the Bay.

4

26   JANE WOLFF

3

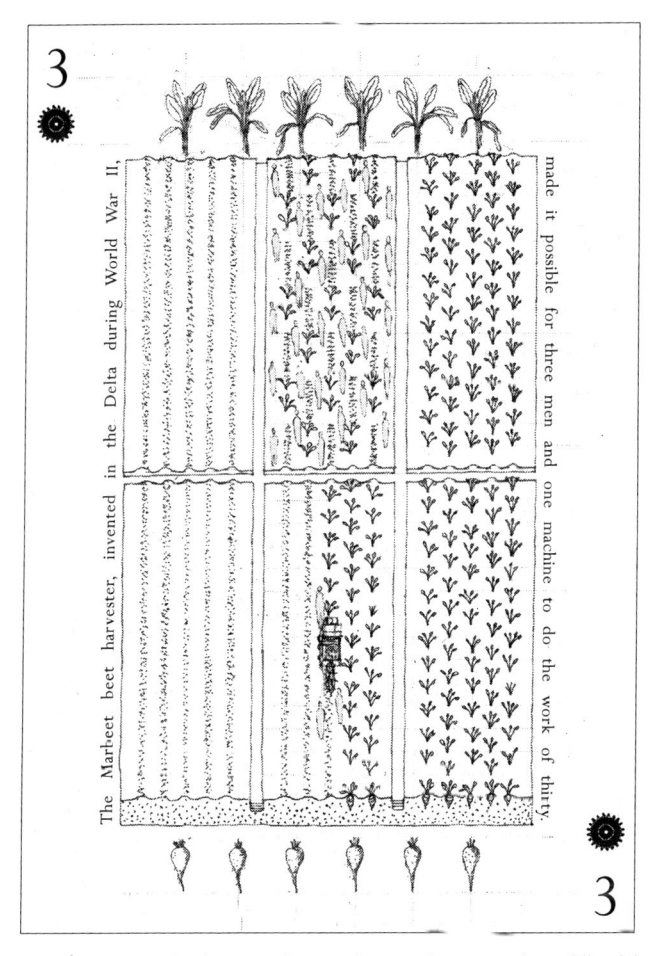

Sugar beets were harvested by hand until the 1940s.

The labor shortage created by World War II inspired Lloyd Schmitt, a Rio Vista welder, to develop a beet harvester. The machine pulled beets from the ground and separated the leaves from the roots. Made by the Blackwelder Company of Rio Vista, it went into use all over the United States.

The Marbeet beet harvester, invented in the Delta during World War II, made it possible for three men and one machine to do the work of thirty.

3

Mr. Schmitt's harvester was the product of tinkering and practicality. His shop was in the middle of the beet fields, and his intimate knowledge of the situation helped him find a solution that had eluded engineers from the agriculture school at Davis. His modest invention, developed from materials he had at hand, transformed beet cultivation in the Delta and across the country.

9

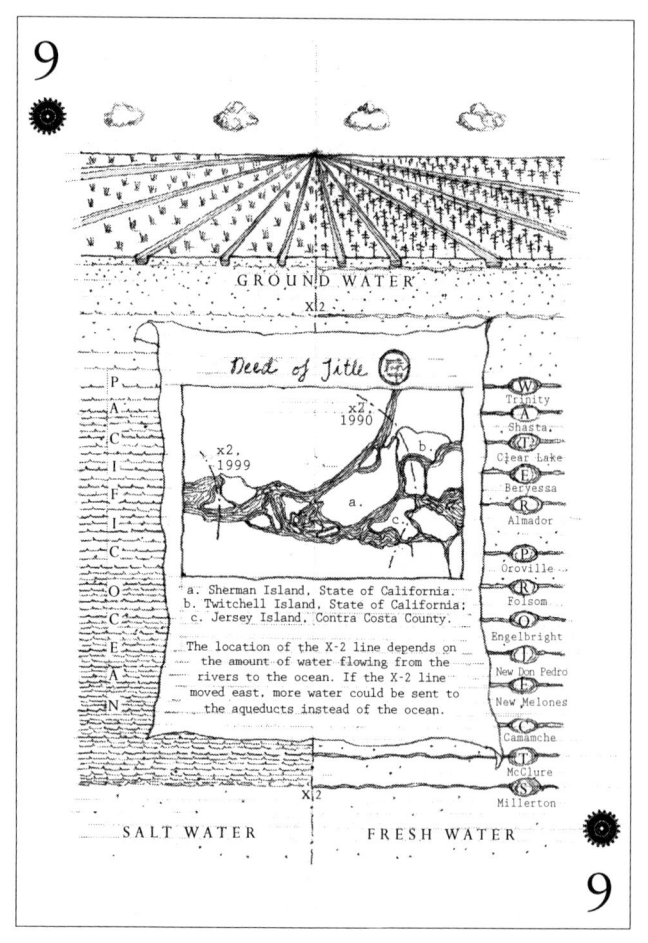

Deed of Title

a. Sherman Island, State of California.
b. Twitchell Island, State of California;
c. Jersey Island, Contra Costa County.

The location of the X-2 line depends on the amount of water flowing from the rivers to the ocean. If the X-2 line moved east, more water could be sent to the aqueducts instead of the ocean.

PACIFIC OCEAN

GROUND WATER
x2

SALT WATER | FRESH WATER

Trinity, Shasta, Clear Lake, Beryessa, Almador, Oroville, Folsom, Engelbright, New Don Pedro, New Melones, Camanche, McClure, Millerton

The quality of the groundwater moving through the Delta depends on its relation to the X-2 line, where salty water from the bay meets fresh water from the rivers. The location of the X-2 line depends on the amount of water released from dams upstream and on the amount of water diverted from the rivers to the aqueducts. By buying land at the mouth of the Delta, the state absolves itself of the responsibility to maintain fresh water for the owners of farm land. Less water needs to flow west; more can be sent south. Land ownership has become a tool for the allocation of water.

JANE WOLFF

8

Cultivation takes different forms at the Cosumnes River Preserve. Some of the land is used for sustainable agriculture, and the rest is devoted to raising wetlands.

At the Cosumnes River Nature Preserve the Nature Conservancy is transforming farm land at the river's edge to native wetland and grassland habitat and cultivating other land seasonally.

8

Managed to present an image of nature, the Preserve is for humans as much as plants and animals. People go there to take walks, or watch birds, or canoe, or plant native oak trees

JANE WOLFF

10

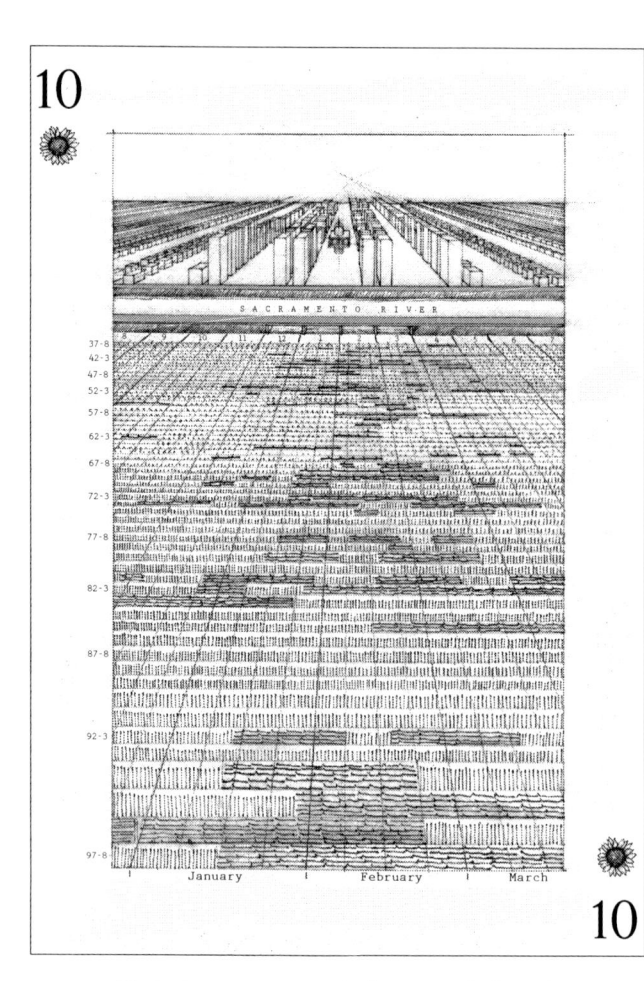

The Yolo Bypass is productive land in more than one way. Most of the time it can be farmed. When flooding interferes with farming, the bypass provides habitat for wetland birds and it protects the city from high water.

The landscape is a negotiated solution to multiple needs.

30   JANE WOLFF

Monica Regan

from MEASURED IN CIRCLES

coming and going

>past 29 palms the map is smooth red lines doubled around black circle towns larger solid dots for cities far away blue lines over white desert roads vein out tunnel through dark string sulpher lights around mountains the wires quake in the wind

>side road along the 40 small white houses stand straight against the blacktop a woman with dark hair carries plastic safeway bags through the side door sets them on an orange counter under oak stained cabinets in late january light down the walk a winter garden dried stalks and hard clods of earth the bees are asleep in their little house

miles

and still
      a wish stuck in the throat

the way your tongue stayed purple
for hours

(wad of wrappers melted together in the back seat)

climbing outside Flagstaff:
someone's swimming pool
strapped to a flatbed

ladder into the deep end
      painted curvy red
           and yellow

grit
on teeth and insides of elbows

    (we hear it)
in the cassette player

roadside stand

man with missing teeth says
           warm today

inside, row of jars: tomatoes, pigs feet
things to put in pies

(a ladder and a red arrow   climbing for the
third try   other girls had cross backed suits
chewed juicy fruit in time with the slap of
orange and pink flip flops their mothers bought
at the corner 5 and dime   grit from the black
no-slip strips on the steps   eyes closed
fingers pressed flat   three breaths and
go)

Loren Chasse

from Site sonologies

> "There are times when I am so compelled by a sonic detail of the city that I suspend the purposefulness of my walk and surrender my ears to the moment. Imaginably, a strange clock of sounds exists in the interstices of the seasons, days and seconds. A sound in intervals coursing through the exposed pipes of a building. Timed sprinklers sputtering and hissing. Playgrounds, bells, refrigeration droning, grates rumbling, the soughing of hidden treelines, hounds under influence of a full moon. Imaginably, we could draw a map of this ambient city"

site sonology #1
sutro baths
ocean beach
9/2/01   4pm

I arrive at the baths around 3pm on Sunday and wander about making audio recordings ...... scraps of conversation, laughter, birds, dogs, surf, footsteps crunching gravel, fog horns, belled buoys, a tour bus hovering ....

The two friends of mine who have come along improvise songs with guitars, bells and xylophones in a central part of the ruins. Various 'audiences' gather at different times, but mostly the people strolling about the ruins are indifferent to the spectacle of our noises.

A woman and man, wrapped in a blanket, request a 'love song' and my friends oblige with a pulse of bells and chords in return for the couple's permission to let me take their picture cuddling on a rock during the song.

A man comes over to the top edge of a wall below which I am sitting and comments, ambiguously: *It sounded like shit from up there so I thought I'd come down to check it out.*

Later, in another area of the ruins I ground small pieces of soft black rock with a large chunk of cement, amplifying this action with a contact microphone and battery-operated speaker.

Lastly, from several cassette players concealed in a slope of iceplants along the path, I amplify recordings made from areas along Ocean Beach over the past few months. This collage includes much surf noise and durations in which children are playing excitedly in the sand. I observe from a distance as one passerby self-consciously tries to find the source of these sounds. He pokes around at a tape player for a moment and then continues on down the path and into the tunnel.

site sonology #2
pedestrian tunnel
golden gate park
9/9/01   10am

I arrive at the tunnel at 9:45 on a damp and foggy morning. About a dozen workmen are busy loading trucks with debris at the far end of the Academy service road while fifteen to twenty people are practicing Tai Chi in the central courtyard on the lawn between the fountains. Inside the tunnel, trails of mud and dried leaves run the length of each wall.

I begin by recording the local ambience from inside the tunnel, the vaulted chamber becoming a sort of crude resonator for the intermittent sounds of rubble falling from barrels into truck containers, hollers, the hiss of fountain water, birds, dogs, whistles and wind.

With a small rock from the tunnel floor, I walk the length of the tunnel several times while continuously scraping the stucco ceiling, my feet sporadically traipsing through and crunching the large crab-shaped leaves.

Then I amplify an edit of the recordings I had made from Sutro Baths (site sonology #1), concealing the speaker beneath a pile of leaves near one end of the tunnel. At the other end I set up a small amplifier and by specifically positioning a contact microphone beneath a large stone, I generate a pulsating feedback pattern.

During this time (about twenty minutes), no pedestrians come through. I do see, however, several pairs of legs at different times stopped above the south entrance to the tunnel, as if observing/listening. I realize that my activities might seem a little strange and could very well discourage people from walking in.

I decide to move on to something more 'accessible'. I continuously strike a bell with a mallet, slowly changing my position within the tunnel. Not long into this, I hear a discussion from outside the south end of the tunnel. The voices of two children and a man:
"What's he doing in there?"
"It sounds like he's ringing a bell."
"Can we go in and see?"
"I don't see why not."
They come in and we have a short conversation about my purpose there. The children ask to ring the bell.

I leave the site at nearly eleven.

Albert Flynn DeSilver

FOR MAXIMUS

>
> Spring was at the hems, the helm of,
> >
> > a man walking the
> >
> > sea point, The
>
> Cut, the
> >
> > half bank, the
> >
> > rocks that the tides
> > >
> > > devoured—

and there he mused
>
> —himself— to himself
> >
> > a map at half mast
> > >
> > > once,
> >
> > and then a chart
> > >
> > > of the Atlantic bottom, open

in reverse;
>
> (sea revines, choppy depth, incised earth—
> >
> > drowned then shed)

at one with his skin,
>
> the sky above Gloucester,
> >
> > billowing
> > >
> > > him forward.

Edric Mesmer

Arendt's law

>> red occupying polygon
>>> shaped redness

> if of or for pangaeic
>> do we mean before or after?

>> or danger offers ideology
>> not if STOP

> for octagon in sign is "purely
>> imaginary distinction" of red

>> "pseudo-mystical" if of or for
>>> imperial red

travel often interpreted this signage
circumscribing regal tetragons

>> familial if throng is of mass or
>> station for a crowd its plaza

yellow light wild code

OLIVE LULLABY

    octa   hexa   octa
    hexo   octa   hexo
    octo   hexo   octo
    hexa   octo   hexa

inlay of tone in violet
crisscrossing nightscapes like a polygraph

copper to Copenhagen   copper & so on
in time true midnight—redness drawn nearer

to non-acolytes
authority entwining the taxonomic

                ignorant of modest if peculiar lunules
                    numerals web nereidically

acts of the moon's notion lent the tenets to a
coordinate novelty

zebraic viols play without patent as
genotype scores heavily the valentine of harlequin

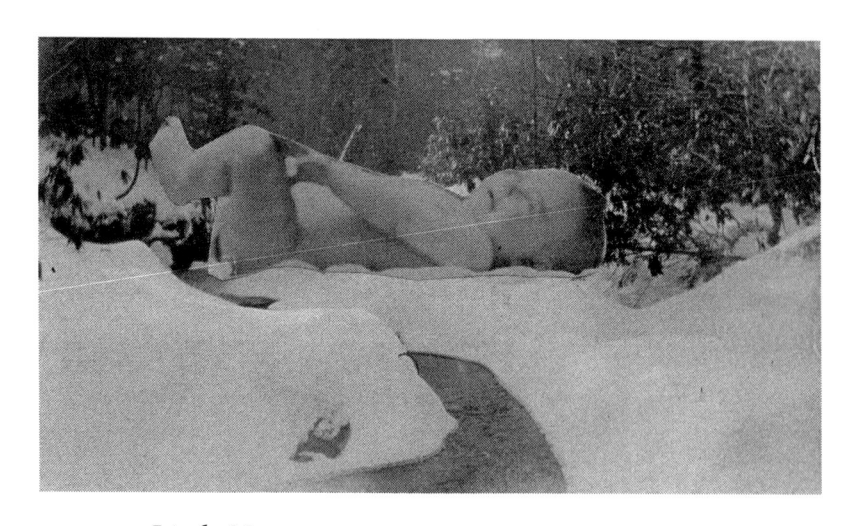

Linda Norton
THE FEN

Laura Sims

Democracy

One verdant minute
after the next, the love of the people
eludes him.

What does it mean? One thing unfolds

as a chain of things: the failure of making
a fantasy park
out of war

in an armchair,
the passage of hundreds of years

the loss of perpetual motion, the line
that proceeds
         "a dark sky, and nothing but fire"
in his absence, the absence
of millions.

Suffering Succotash

    All dead men
    In the mercury dust of spring
    In particular
    Those who were felled
    In one patch of highway scrub brush & trees

    This regime, or a _____ one

    We have never been happier
    Shedding our clothes than we were
    That evening you mention. The silty light
    And it flattened our skin tone and hair.

Eric Selland

from TABLE OF PRIMARIES

A theme I have always played. He lived within the protective confines of an assumed normality. Like a man carrying a secret identity, he passed through the streets performing his daily routine. A series of false starts. A truth that resists in revealing. The life of the house. The sensation such that this would be completely human. The two types appearing in the dream. In the nameless city. The figure in the dream unattainable. The human reality of the present in all its brokenness. And that moment in time framed by his sudden departure. And the cold light of residence. The dark recesses of the house.

It begins with habitation.
Things are apprehended as solid substances.
The requirement that everyone speak was dropped.
The movements of birds and their hidden meanings.

Some lost work has been reconstituted more or less unchanged.
A cartographic mural made of paint and industrial tape.
I am finding I belong to neither world.
The movement comes from without.

The poverty of being in between these two selves, these two times. And yet which in itself was a kind of absence. My life is a whole series of contradictions. Again I dream of C. To think there was a time when all the oppositions came together in one comprehensive whole—a great matrix of ideals and activity. Things fall apart. The image in various stages of disappearance. More and more I am absorbed in K's world. Of this there are signs. The once calm surface becomes disturbed. It is not enough to speak of proximity. Assuming one would want to keep up any correspondence at all. But this, too, has its difficulties.

Loren Chasse

site sonology #3
bunker cranston/battery east rd.
presidio (west of golden gate bridge)
9/16/01   12pm

I had imagined what this event would 'sound' like only because I have explored this site several times over the past years and I have a sort of familiarity with the 'instrument'. What I remember of it is that the bunker is built into a slope so that its slightly-angled roof rises from ground level (ice plants and dust along a ridge that allows a view of the Bridge and the entrance to the Bay) on its ocean-facing side and is accessible on its inland side from several staircases that lead down to a paved walkway running along a long wall quartered by massive steel doors. Through one or more of these ajar doors you can enter the bunker and step among broken glass, feathers, garbage, sticks and chunks of masonry. Today I set out with a harmonium, a small amplifier and some recordings from this and other California bunkers that I have compiled over the years. Also, I bring with me some contact mics and a violin bow to be used somehow with the doors and the bars on the windows.

Nearing the entrance to the Bridge on Sunday I notice that many of the roads leading to various landmarks and trailheads in the Presidio are closed off and guarded by the police. Battery East Rd. is among these sealed-off areas and so the bunker is not accessible.

Of course, this is all part of a great precaution being taken around a significant feature of San Francisco that, imaginably, has become a potential target for terrorism. I end up crossing the Bridge and spending the day in Marin, the harmonium coming out briefly and without inspiration in a pull-off along Route One.

This probably qualifies as the first 'implied' performance in my series.

Erica Bernheim

Pavese Said Death Will Come Bearing Your Eyes

It is late at night
and you are making
soup for other people.
There are wool sweaters
in piles around your
ankles and your nose
seems full of blood.
A little boy brought
a newspaper for you
today; it was bright
and cold. You were
thick and unlovely until
your body hit the
water. Now. When cops
lie, you call it the
blue wall. You will
develop a great true
love for the metronomes,
placing them on the
shelves of your closets,
keeping track of your
frequently silent comings.
Automatic, quiet, more

of everything. When the
season begins, these
girls you know will all
buy Bibles, creatures of
habit. You are not
ready for a reunion,
whatever it is. Who-
ever made this room
knew his flashes of
brilliance wouldn't last
much longer, so he
painted in huge colors
and couldn't bring himself
to buy a watch, your
father's dead, and it
is late. Even
dishonest people become
involved in terribly
disappointing ventures,
and you say this is one,
this is for your grace.

kari edwards

A TRUMPETING THEME SONG

I tried to set it straight – turn the proper thick sound into a bird song, no bird this side of shadow town could sing. play it tall. obey the laws; no left turn on off days. follow the bouncing ball, repeat after me: "do no go to the same sanatorium as cocteau, talk to blake on someone else's doormat, only accept collect calls from screaming banshees i.e., jean d'arc, julian of norwich, sappho, abigail adams, and mary shelley...." none of this, "hello, is this mr. or miss_____" heads bumped, then lost at home in most instances and despite it all, under an unwritten code of ethics somewhere on the other side of the same place, miles away from embarrassment for a mother or second rate monet or first rate mary cassatt (not to compare the two or three).

a war rages, is about to rage, is on the rampage, beats its drum, recovers from crimes of, acts of, trials of, rehabilitations of, history of, deep in the ashes, bones and snake oil slick, medals pinned, victory parades. bits and pieces arrive, identified as the aforementioned foreskin of_____ or the left hook of the deceased.

there's bats in the beltway and a cat's eye refocuses to a cry from a late missed show on continuous repeat. no more skips, just bits of dust in a laser beam ... "scotty, it's time, take us home."

or

the romulans are about to attack

or

disturb as little as possible

or

this land is your land . . . .

or

sit up and take notice, somewhere there is a sound that is not human.

APPLICATIONS WILL BE ACKNOWLEDGED

I had a thought in lower case letters. it should have been capitalized with its sum laid out the way the homeless are after an election. a luminous gray threw solid bodies at me, stacking in the muddy paths of history. as soon as I looked at a place behind the counter, I became a collector's item with dealers from around the world reading my signs for suicidal tendencies. later I debriefed myself over cocktails and an exit worth noting. at first, it was the language, then it was pigs with peg legs, then a diary of an attic dweller. I called m. for a feeling and the thought my brain had left. someone had written "your self whole heartedly" and someone else had said " maybe we should go there." as they say, "one turn is another's dresser," so, I considered suicide, but the price had dropped, was rehashed and condensed instead at $75.00 an hour. I became poured cement. the condition was this side of beelzebub (another otherwise object with deadpan humor). I remained an object which listened to absence and counted the way to shortened things spelled correctly.

David Harrison Horton

from Bei Hai: North of the Sea

For this, I am my own companion. Vehicles and buildings. Uniformed parasols. Sweeps away the refuse, but the street is not clean. He carries a heavy load. Mustn't be shirked. Sweat down his back. Marx and sandwiches; Jesus and bread. Beach scent without scenery. A quarrel over pricing. The Five Heroes of Wolf's Teeth Mountain. This or that mistake. A true intention. Figurines and laquerwork; rice among the lotus. A haze. A fog. The difference. Rowed accommodations. Ko Chen-li the first mentioned. What he fought for. Where he fell. Again, the shore is no different than other shores. A city. A collection. Vendors here hock fish, fuzzy clawed crab. The laoban will walk with you. Give some direction. Get xiaojie to knock at the door. Boats and lures. Potentially two oceans. A concrete dock. An aluminum globe. An atrocity of architectures. A strip of sand that is adequate. A vessel on the ready. Shakespeare and Eliot; a convalescence. Of dubious binding. Late coming. Flow of fishes. Men less adept. In the sea all men are gods. An order. St. James, patron of sailors. Shells and mussels. Diffused ray. Ships without flags; a short destination. One code for the sea; one for land. Fresh and salt waters combined. A filament. Lords we accept. Blood of blood of blood before us. The sea has no such qualms. Tides are that weeps. Bereft. A struggle for dignity. Its end. There are no apologies among men; gods. Things are. It has always been. Shipworthy. A breach. Skeletons. A scavenge. False horizon. A time on the clock. The shore is a slow birthing. Carpet woven by hand. Being has a dignity; existence is higher. Come again the seasons. A rote. Withstand; merits of meaning. What one does not know. Boats aligned; soldiers. A track one cannot follow. A victory, if subtle. Bells and foliage. The mosque is over there, the church there. To get around the city. Covers the ground you walk on. The things one cannot see. A city in darkness; a darkness disturbed. Factory. The middle heart is never emptied. Witness to perpetuity. Bait and salt among the citrus. Faculties amended. When I walk down this alley I find nothing of interest. Endemic. Vertical. Rats in the harbor. Unfinished business. Palm and bamboo. Close and distant. Defined channels. Manlike. Not gods. A subjection of chaos. A system. Routine. What is given. What is created. The hell for heroes, not gods. An acceptance. To cry as Whitman did, or Isaiah. There is lack here. Deep rooted lack. A need to please. A cowardice. Whether the cattle be oxen or steer makes no difference. A hand held high as in authority. An interior precipice. Self-disclosure. The limit to what one can know. A country is another's idea. Not the self. Consanguinity. Ill-fit heritage. An unsteady faultline. A chasm. There is no patchwork to be done. Avow or repudiate. The breasts that suckle slaves. Reversal of decision. Impotence met with a faultering. Hu Fu-tsai determined. Irrevocable an action. Actors on a shod built set. A desecrated temple. Archetype. Beholden. A time well within. Feudalism demarcated. Absolution. A communal well. A well-walked road. Not intrinsic. Capitulated. A line of hosts and at the head. Kowtow. Concern of this or that the other. Elder statesmen graveside. Begonias. There is no word that all men know. Of human form. Forbearance. Condensation on cut glass. The desert is never far, not here. The drought that eat waters. Cratered path; higher truths sustain. This is an age among many. There came invasion. Proscription. A cost. Detriment. Below the trees above the soil, mayhem. He that would. Abdicate. A queen for hunger. Mixed waters a tide. Let shepherds their meek way go, abiding seasons. To originate nothing. A death entire. Fastidious. Days and men may die but not the will. A turning point. An agitation. Thought through. Reconsidered. Hecate at the gate. The need for heroes admits a weakness. Subtlety of undertow. Surrounded by externals. Shell cobbled. When she smiles, it is a formality, manlike. A reason upheld that does not necessitate. A drop in the ocean. The need of a line. Differentiation. Values assigned where not necessary. Things are. This or that tomb; a sleeping city. Conquest of Paris. All the omens. An aqueduct, a bridge. Convention. The high halls of Hrothgar; the aftermath. If not this age perhaps the next. Cemetery filled with flowers. Stones above cut horizon. Mills and mortice. Philomath. To bear the brunt. Corroborate. To walk in none other's shoes but your own. The city is not dead. It has never lived. Movement without pulse. Mechanical. A shuttling from here to there; mimic of action. Unbetrothed. The other kingdom is not a god's concern. Means very little. Hu Tsc-lin's hell is not a concern. Means nothing. He that came before. He to come after. Not in this age. The bones of Elisha and Elijah. The desert encroaches the city. Dustbowl. This or that stamp. Acquiescence. Frugality of merit. Terse reflection. Bullets and ballots. To see into the life of things. Slight and trivial influence. Held up. Fakeries of action. Confounded. A blue or grey sky does not change matters. Wars and destruction; the force of will. One need not follow. The type and symbol of eternity. Altercate. Alacrity in reason. Point fixed beyond the shore. At the center only merged forms. The source of waking dreams. Imprecision. A hesitant step that does define. The unnamed at Chessboard Slope. A river proudly bridged. The thoughts of women among men. Rice in the field. Abnegate concession. Architecture a tale of falsity. Dominion. Every inhabited place a lie. A boar's back. Full stop. Men among gods. The weakness. Admetus, his shame. To cower on the footpath, death already. Sand beaten into glass. To stare fixated upon the distance, to be blind. A disrobing. Infection without cure. An ocean of one's self. If not understood, then nothing. No race or merit. Collapsed façade. Colonial. A true inheritance. A series. A string. A beetle's strength; a tired turtle. Dredged canals; highways of a second order. To return to a point is to drown. Moribund. Boethius. The cut of the cowl makes no difference. The rhythm and sound of true life. Behest. Antiquated. The relics of the past are dust or decayed. Models of frailty. The stumbling block is not the Christ but vision. A man confused is blind. Shylock's blood is human blood but limited. A Pilate portrayed cowardlike. Atuned to time and place. The blindness brought on by the sea. The initial state. Each choice a direction; new path. A voice that does not carry.

Andrew Felsinger

Hysterical Materialism

> The booming flowers are an affect of local politics
> Just as the bed sheets are torn to assure us peace
> Thusly we misidentify ourselves as a cannon
> And a gaffe is made to turn its back
> Like the sky flung across the neck of a welcoming nude
> Each cylinder, orchid, thread, furnace
> Has time and thought at its most real
> For as the screaming quiets the neighborhood
> The melon is cut.

Jennifer Scappettone

…from the Time of the Royal Tombs of Ur

4. Kilted Hero Attacking Felines Menacing Horned Animals; Human-Headed Bull Below Empty Space

>It's November, and I'm not here again
>sealing wounds; dealing in dawn; in code yaw

1. Lion Menacing Bull Man Grasping Ibex; Gazelle Held by Nude Hero

>Despite every guarantee; my father
>specializes in the ages of things; beheld

6. Banquet Scene; Eagle Clutching Antelopes

>Runaway awake at all angles
>whose awkward tupperwares, strategic mess

7. Seated Figures Drinking Through Tubes in a Vessel. Eagle Between Small Animals with a Boar and a Scorpion

>Hoarse sucking rite loose
>no name to make it romance. Some mascot omen

8. Attendant Between Seated Woman and Man Each Raising a Beaker

> Overseen betweens ubiquitous in glass case
> escapes pellmell annals

9. Feline, with Plough Above, Before Boat with Seated Deity Propelled by Human Prow; Small Bird Behind Lion-Headed Stern

> Whose doors have lost their clay
> as idiolect agape over

12. God with a Mace Presenting Female Toward Enthroned God with Attendant

> Here no pastel elder. What stays is urge's inert origin;
> and familiar

2. Heroes Protecting Animals from Felines; Inscribed, Prince (?)...of Uruk

> I saw he came and left, leaving nothing
> we would not want

Mark Wallace

from Belief Is Impossible

2)
From what angle to consider
how people fill a room? Compensation
is no compensation. The city night
still lacks a schedule. I don't say much anymore

about who I think I am. At that hour
one can't drive against the traffic.
You said you thought you knew me.
I said I thought so too.

5)
You may be right, but nobody
likes you. Everybody likes you
but you're not right. Poetry contains
a lot of things that are not poetry.

Gain is not the goal of love
but poverty can make love impossible.
Let's help each other know what we want
and what we want to know, and how to know it.

16)
In a city like this, friends
aren't easy to find. She said it was time

to think about leaving. Anonymity
can be freeing or crushing. Hand me the door.

With my windows open, trucks on the street are loud
at all times. Performance is metaphor
but that doesn't mean we don't live it.
I'm tired of hearing about the highway.

17)
Starved for an aura, a man peers
in the institute doorway. The weight
of production presses on the night.
All our lives we've been told

what we can't do. Looking for Medusa,
the committee finally filed its findings
to be continued. The aesthetic of bureaucracy
calls on the phone when a woman dims a lamp.

22)
Patterns of wind inside the room
are not deceptions that lead to enlightenment.
The more history I have, the stranger
each past seems. We've had a rainy

friendship. It's not like one has to look
for irony. Lights on the sides of buildings
are not warning signals. I startled
when the blinds hit the windows.

Loren Chasse

site sonology #4
spofford alley
chinatown
10/4/01 6pm

I came upon this alley during my first visit to Chinatown nine years ago. Over the years, on each of my subsequent walks along this single block it has felt as if it is at the heart of a community. Like many locations in any city, this 'site' is so particularly evocative of the imagination. Gates and doorways, partially opened, allow glimpses of interiors and stairways leading in different directions. The windows of the upper floors are set in old brick, their angles and edges obliterated from erosion, and details of domestic activities and personalities are precariously situated on the sills. Outlines of individuals hang from clotheslines. Through some windows candlelight makes shadows flicker and smoke carries smells of incense and cooking to the street.

Because I am not a resident of this neighborhood and because I am not part of the Chinese community, the mysteries of Spofford Alley are heightened a little. I cannot read the signs and I cannot take direct meaning from the conversations I overhear. Above the large curtained shop windows along street level are rows of narrow transom windows, most of which are open. Each time I have been here, I have heard frantic clattering and bristling emanate from these openings. Additionally, like sounds resonate in the stairwells leading below street level. If you peer through many of the gates, most of which are latched and accompanied by dirty white buzzers, you can often see corners and edges of cardtables, wrists extending from cuffs, some fingers moving rapidly across areas of white blocks and tiny wooden rods, shuffling and positioning them, more slowly moving among ashtrays, purses, and soda cans. Over the years I have always enjoyed the ambience of these Mah-Jong gaming parlors, noticing how this sound provides a unique bed for the racket of the city to lie down on.

While the 'performance' here is completely implied, the sound itself certainly is not. I imagine how anyone patient enough to commute to Chinatown and look for this obscure site will immediately recognize what he/she had come for. On the last day of this 'scheduled' event I did show up to make some recordings and take pictures. At nearly 6:30 close to a dozen children on rollerskates appeared at one end of the alley and contributed a fabulous layer of noise to the site as they repeatedly skated from one end to the other, giggling and singing the whole time.

Anthony Hawley

Icefield Sonnets

    1.
Cold is a cell
In which one is allowed

To walk around the lake
And think of walking

Or defend the logic
Of glacier water

Sing the oval
With a skate's blade

Habits of its shape
The way a lip

Leaves an imprint
On glass a trace

Air enough just
To shake the frame

2.
Glass is a place
From which to view

Withinwithout
Say hellogoodbye

In the same line
Or move across

An icy surface
Inches forward

Years witness
Little change

Requires a fixed gaze
To observe glacial

Motion the elk
Make stirrings

3.
North is a notion
And a motion tundra's

Stilled grammar
Or the beauty of scant

And drowned out
Reverberate

Throughout the town
Built in planks round

About the river forks
The mouth's glissade

In which direction
Doesn't matter

There's north enough
To keep lips frozen

Elizabeth Willis

ENCHANTER'S NIGHTSHADE

Sunk into silver, I can't quite organize my hand. The overhead eye pinks the moaning train. Everything sea-like refers to you, you have a number, taxi-like, a pro. I couldn't be later, couldn't see over the hedge or think to regret the clammy hand on my cheeky wisdom. Cherries flood the bordertowns, with curves like salty jetties, faced and sweeping. If I don't go now I'll never reach Tulsa, crawling by rowboat or even on your back.

Female figs supposed to be monsters

When I tasted the cookie I couldn't go back. Even the closing door was a quake upon these lacy nerves. The picture in your locker flapped against my squeaky air. If I could borrow your hookah for only a day, or wobble down the gravel walk in someone else's bucks. I was sinking in the basement pool when your shadow woke me up. Aeschylus as untranslatable as absinthe, my Ishmael was lost. Why so grave upon the deep? The biggest white forehead is steaming past the cape, puffing out the century with asthma and brocade.

Meteoric flowers

Girl is notational, she's an index. From the couch I see Mary saying yes and no, he and she. We're only clay. Blossom machines. Sure, I'll carry your latest worry, sorry if it's not dripping in your favorite green. I love the shady elm, my dear, but how long can it hide us? Our cheeks are marked with leafy stains. What lasts forever won't survive its station any more than that junebug can translate through the screen. We're living on, anyway, immaculate lawns. Neo-forsythia.

Edwin Torres

The Myth of a Popular Distance (*after Gustave Flaubert*)

1

The master of secrets—believes in the power
to use story, as punctured sky lit by death,
transformed by symbol

> The Sadistic Comet of The Mind
> The Origin of Myth
> The animal who cannot speak like a man
> The shadow of his speaking
> Mythos as Mute
> Medusa as Right Blood > Poison
>   Left Blood > Love

Death is connected
to the divine level mystering in my work
No one reminds me of these games
and their ultimate creation through enigma
Self's seperation is transformation's dawn

> An arrow with its points
>   breaking around me
> A star whose field
>   becomes my story

In the memory of empty catastrophe
In the island of fissures
the hands of the ocean prevent the fisherman
from reaching his shores
Landing on broken answers,
it's possible to imagine—a lace of hands
profoundly pointed
to broken stars

You are my slight detour, sitting next to me
painting the world without fear, skyless and high
a brush for your arms
In the years between my questions
crush my napkin, put it in a cup
hold it and let me drink my empty hands

You are the starting point of my secrets
the end of silent air
Taking an attachment
using it to attack—in a killing life

Using killing as a life, that span of time
a reproducible murder
over the reach of suffering
writing itself over and over

A poet has only one thing to write
and does so for the lifespan of the poet
the one thing is—the writing

Singular and infinite
the poet writes the poet
over and over

11
Dare to reveal
and leave yourself dared—or at least
regretted
Give yourself that which you dare
it leads to decisions at key momentum droppings

To kiss or kill—
disection of this writing
Castrating poet, brutal alchemist
in search of perfect word

Undaunted by hubub, unfullfilled by fate—
this connection attempts a shared passage
A breakthrough
for those who want to be broken

My immediate space
is here
between betweens
that direct space into disection

Frankenstonian: my life is not
consist of event,s

of thought,s it, is, my fantasia is,
conversia ultimate

the phantom's pantomime
Epileptic hobo: body contort
creating a symptom to escape life—the unsayable,
a symbol for death, a replacement

III
Oedipal constellation
Ejaculation of memory
Images jerked in hallucination
A thousand symbols
Erupting into consciousness

The father cures the illness brought on by the father
by doing that which is only allowable by the diseaser, to die
Allowing the son his only remedy—to be with the mother—
the son seeks revenge for giving him bite marks
by constantly dying in front of her
intersecting castration with self, gazing forward by inward chaos
father makes life real by dying at hands of materials—
an artist of life, realizing his vision

> I saw a man who was the confession between
> father and brother, a symbolic representation
> of lover as dead language
> I saw a man who was the anniversary of his birth,

a death candle as research into ambiguous ambiguity
I saw a man who was an external repression,
an installation of transformed relationships, an architecture of privacy
I saw a man linked to a gashed painting torn from sky
knifed onto earth, a reflective participant as a scar of his time
I saw a man who was inviting carressing and touching,
a symbolic cemetary composed of a future
that could not happen, a cementing of hands
inscribed on memory, in flavors I can't pronounce
presented by nowness and thoughts, meant to impress

If this building is a story
it is a height called up from carbon's essence
If I combine these stories
do I read an impulse into connection
do I feel well enough in my good architecture for such privacy
Rewarded by emotion of morning, soul
is more than I can say

Failing to ignite, what you do
stays on earth, what you see is a series of mistakes
below the failure—ascend to the surface, you'll see eternity—
my accomplice to complexity

> This is my attempt to relate to the sun
> with a series of cuts—I am a visitor
> of places without fear, faceless without fear
> I am here in your arms
> your distance as loud as mine

IV
This is in memory of the disappeared ones
the missing who haven't been
those who once were never, and that
which hasn't yet become

This is a text, commemorating that
which hasn't been written, meant
to be invisible as you read it, these very words
are not here, a celebration of memory
the beginning of disappearance

Experience as absence
creation implied, overcoming
loss—not every space occupied,
a mapping of the area, spreading out
over all you can, but—in your own time
Scribbles that slowly fill the page, but each line
its own dimension

This is the voice just becoming
that is not yet a voice, a particular negotiation
of closeness with stillness, one of humankind's
oldest structures—the architecture of one's space
All levels of perception, look closer
and toward it,
walk on it—and let yourself, possibly, enter

He was only another dust-cloud of the sultry sameness.
darkness
rose out
speeding
after a struggle of hours

The night passed, the morning came
in the afternoon
That one day was the sun of his life.

the books, pamphlets, trinkets,
hair, thin
plays of the union
at the curtain

like a lighted brand
upon surrounding images
like a dried channel of tears
of herself
such sprawling skeletons
bath at the
vexation

texts of
the unconscious colour
O God!

short black
ghost of
eyes

garden of no
breathing structure

He was down on the plains
and he stood there like vividness
sparkling over her sex
to keep the world alive

But she was inanimate
the room was black and silent
tyrannized with the mask of
both

And
the brain
pulses the ghosts
with emptiness
while the snow wishes its wish

Brandon Downing
CXXIX *from* LAKE ANTIQUITY

and
the young
kick the water to kill,

Laura Walker

SIX PORTRAITS OF THE LETTER B

one
as a small (page)
might expand might
(turn) elizabeth
washing the ends of
her braids where
(they) had dipped in paint

two
fish unhooked a bruise
a boy whose (hook)
must absorb largely
we find him in storybook
pages his bandana briefly
and torn

three
a choke hold a choke (risk) a
(leaf) dipped in butter she
uses them as tiny boats she
waves them on the page

four
the smell of stitches (cloth)
to carry as in she (once)
wore the bear's head once
(the spackled bells)

five
beads beaks a straw to soak thin
(this bathtub and after) the reeds
(   )
her littlest temperatures rise

six
incredible aspirations (as if
you must blow this seed from
this letter) she tore bright
stairs to shreds

Trina Baker

The Pilgrim Stumbles

      1) Not at home
      you take to the street
      go back go back go back

7) So you take to your feet
and know where you are some-
where between Second and Broadway.

      2) But the key no longer
      fits and the tumblers
      don't turn won't turn

6) You park the car and
check the map
wrong map wrong map wrong map

      3) Pick a car
      something hot and red and
      don't look back look back

  5) And don't stop
  for anything but the
  word *alpha* and the word *omega*

      4) Though the wheels spin
      on the freeway and say wrong
      road wrong road wrong road

Ben Lerner

from The Lichtenberg Figures

for Benjamin

The forgetting begins.
Infinitives are hewn from events.
The letters of your name fall asleep at their posts.
The dead vote in new members. Police declaw your books.

A suspicious white powder is mailed to the past,
forcing its closure. In order to avoid exposure,
I use the present tense. Sense grows sentimental
at the prospect of deferral. The stars dehisce.

By 'stars' I mean, of course, tradition,
and by 'tradition' I mean nothing at all.
A pronoun disembowels his antecedent.
Stop me if you've heard this one before.

Your body is broken by exegesis.
The thinkable goes sobbing door to door.

for Benjamin

The thinkable goes sobbing door to door
in search of predicates accessible by foot.
But sense is much shorter in person
and retreats from chamber to antechamber to text.

How then to structure a premise like a promise?

The heroic negativity of pleasure
is that it makes my body painfully apparent,
a body that weighs six hundred pounds on Jupiter
and next to nothing here in Europe.

How then to justify our margins?

Some cultures use quotation marks for warmth.
In ours they've withered without falling off.
The trees apologize each autumn,
but nature can never be sorry enough.

Loren Chasse

site sonology #5
vulcan staircase (at ord st.)
the castro
10/21/01   2pm

  The public staircases characteristic of this 'steep' neighborhood above the Castro give pedestrians access to intimacies of the neighborhood usually reserved for residents whose backyards adjoin and whose windows look out into the spaces behind the streets and beyond their noises. The staircase named Vulcan rises up, westward, from Ord St. Its whole length cannot be taken in from this perspective. It climbs through several landings, planted densely and colorfully on either side with dahlias and shrubs and fruit trees, and then makes a turn and disappears into an overhang of branches all seemingly coming down from the skirt of a towering redwood. It is in such places in the city that pedestrians might very easily, with a tilt of the head, eliminate the buildings from their periphery and, in the insular quietude of the setting, frame for themselves a fragment of momentary wilderness.

    Once you climb inside the cover of the overhang, the staircase becomes more private. At first, near the bottom, you step in full view of the house windows that border the gardens along the stairs and there is a slight feeling of trespass. Your voice and footsteps bounce from the concrete and walls. However, once the staircase becomes tunnel-like, ascending through the shadows of hedges and trees, you gain a privacy that is yours alone. From here, your climb takes you past a massive blackberry hedge on one side and various flowering hedges, gates and treelines on the other, obscuring yards and walkways leading to people's homes. Above, branches and vines twist across and mute daylight. In this steeply-angled enclosure, the murmur of dishes and footsteps and conversations, of a book or something sliding across a table, a hinge, something motoring, some plumbing.... resonates and mixes with the birds, the foliage shaking in the wind, the hammering from a backyard and natural bits falling.

Today I bring several strands of bells and hang them in the ends of a large eucalyptus branch I find in a thicket above one of the landings. My 'performance' consists of dragging this branch behind me as I ascend and descend the staircase several times, the instrument hissing and ringing rhythmically from stair to stair, its sound sustained in regular intervals for the duration of each landing. As I pass the first gated walkway, leading to the enclosed porch of a house, I find out just how my action is going to influence the ambience of the neighborhood from there on out..........

Dogs!

Whereas the mere footsteps and voices of pedestrians on the staircase, because of their regularity from day to day, do not seem to evoke any canine attention, the unfamiliar sound of the bells does trigger a chorus of barking from the neighborhood dogs, which inevitably escalates into the hushes and shouts of dog-owners, the slamming of doors and the frenzied clicking and patting of dog nails and paws on various surfaces. Once I bring my branch to a halt, this symptomatic noise runs its course for several minutes before the peaceful thick of things at the staircase is restored.

Linda Norton
MINE

Jack Collom

FIRST SIP OF WINE

    The Word "Save"

AT LAST, PEOPLE CAN	
TOSS AWAY THE ENVIRONMENTAL MOVEMENT ON	
THE GROUNDS	wild rose
THAT THERE ARE WORLDS UPON WORLDS,	
ROLLING THROUGH TIME LIKE BLINKING SPHERES	Queen Anne's Lace
OUT THE WINDOW ON A BUSRIDE,	
AND WHY COP TO THE SENTIMENTAL WISH	yarrow
TO RETAIN THIS PARTICULAR WORLD,	
MADE OF REDTAILS, VIOLETS AND WILD MICE?	chokecherry

Save, save.	chicory
Neither the history of poetry nor the presence of nature	
fits in a plastic box,	salsify
however commodious; maybe we can't	
save them.	prairie phlox

"Save"?	verbena
Maybe to preserve something,	
sprinkle wordsalt on classic fetal curl,	prickly poppy
goes against nature, even though we,	
paradoxically,	evening primrose

hook up the pickled doings to other times
(the word classic is a reference). Matter of   milkweed
links.

                                               sunflower
    If we
    expand that there paradox   asters
    that paradox, to the constancy of change, we can
    see recognition   goldenrod
    as merely an oxygenated circle. We can
    set the transitive to gulping subject, object. thistle
    In such accurate light
    "save"   buckbrush
    stinks.

                                               blue grama grass
Wind up with
a prime axis: bluestems
two prickles on a ball,
like ears on an owl.   switch grass

To preserve (something) in the   pepper grass
face of entropy, to

                                             artemisia
rescue anything from harm (process),
equals a closed system.   peachleaf willow

    Growth and death point up the basic
    museum folly. Folly. Folly Silly paradigm diorama.

    But folly is of the essence,

        for to get outside of all paradigms is simply
        to perish.

                                            box elder
    SAVE contains contains contains all the motion
brains can register. Triangulates.   wild plum
Though   nothing is ever truly saved,
there's nothing else.   golden currant

        (If you're invited to a gesture, don't
        expect Them
        to provide a main dish.)

At "Walden Ponds," for example, east of town, just
west of 75th St.,
save SAVE save SAVE save:
the main one, labeled Cottonwood Marsh,

        (Spill
        And
        Vanish.
        Evanesce!)

Used to be open woods . . . then pasture . . . then
quarried gravel pit, then pond.

Pond is good.
                      Lies
right next to Carl Krucoff's silvery sewage-dome kingdom.

It's a bowl of colorful, plentiful waterfowl —
   pied-billed grebe, white pelican, great blue heron,
      goldeneye, bufflehead, ruddy, pintail — variety's thrill —
         phalarope (spinning), cormorant, Caspian tern,
           plus poignant cries of solitary sandpipers,
              warbles of widgeon. Many more

(Once things can be counted they're almost gone.)

                STOP!
                A!
                Vacant!
                Eternity!

— Something rich about the earth and flowing liquids here (there).

Cattail, teazle swamp surroundings, soon to be (it's February —)
lifebright spring disc: teeming
song sparrows fluttering low,
yellowthroats yodeling "witchery, witchery,"

redwings grinding out organ sounds,
soras appearing suddenly, precipitately, among the stalks,
off the boardwalk.

   "o-ka-lee cong-quer-ree
   you chootea, oolong tea"

JACK COLLOM

Beaver and muskrat, painted turtles, foxes, once a skunk nightrunning
 over my boots.

Bullfrogs. Multiple air-weaving swallows. Sawtooth off west. Moon over
 Long's Peak.

"Sensory sheets lighting up"

... & then arrives at the ponds a beautiful drying-out character (in
 the fall)
 — weed sculpture, Giacometti-like gray-green twists and stretches
as you amble by, heading over to Sawhill (some 20 other precious
 puddles),
 perhaps to curve past the oriole tree,
branchdodge to creek's banks ... what's that blocky shape
 the blue jays won't let sleep?

Et cetera but by now, anno domini 2002, the drying's gone mad,
scouring vitals from this big Walden pond.
Shallowness revealed.
The mud becoming rock-hard and pale.
 — Abstractions of exposure, not of change.
Even the killdeer avoid it.

IN spring when water does return (seasonal,
 off-rhythm)
no more yellow-headed blackbirds squawking there (like French taxis).
No more bitterns (they've pulled up stakes).
Fewer ducks, avocets, egrets dark and light ("fewer"—what a term);

the pond's become a FAScinating WASteland.

"2002" . . . a little omen
of eating own tail?

Magpie cackles, bald eagle circles north . . . crack the whip:
short dragonfly arc.

The Canada geese honk plaintively.
Basin looks like scar-tissue.
Dead-fish phase,
so that there *was* an orgy of plump, white, deceased bellies
   for the ring-billed gulls.
Massive sparkle of wings

> "whip whip the edges of the white
> knife, slightly blurred, the skull of a gull
> leaving slices
> of pale air piled all ricky-tick
> . . .
> in a zigzag barely touching
> sleepy earth"

   for a few minutes.

O—start it up again, the pool of water.
I.e., aiyee, let it drip.

(Shadow falls — osprey flapping by.)

(Shadow, shifting grackle mass.)

(Cowbird shape.)

(Shadow — plane & glider — who's pushing who?)

Part 11

Two years ago I dropped in on the old boyhood woods, ten miles
& a century
west of Chicago.
Got to the point from which we'd (early '40s) head out
over the field to "Bullrush,"
our favorite spot, islet of cottonwoods & (usually) dry mud,
site of many a small campfire . . .
    but the field was gone.

A tall, dense rank of trees stood staring at me
with the same amount of unfamiliarity
that lets a rock act out the infinite
without a face.

> (A little while
> is the only difference between
> poison and delight.)

WHY COP TO THIS WORLD??   green ash
THE ANSWER RANGES LIKE AN ACCORDIONIST'S HAND,
WORKING THE MIDDLE DEVELOPMENT OF TIME —   horsetail
LONGER THAN GREED BUT SHORTER THAN METAPHYSICS —
THE ANSWER'S MADE OF QUESTIONS, LIKE   penstemons

    "WHAT'S WITH GLOBAL FRESHWATER IN 500 YEARS?" buffalo bur
    "HOW MUCH VIABLE SOIL AFTER 1000?"
    "HOW MANY ELEPHANTS MIGHT BE BREATHING,   gumweed
        IN 2020?"
    "CAN YOU WALK UP A HILL OF PROBABILITIES?" AND

"WHO GAVE US THE RIGHT?"
        (Sure, things do what they
        can, but the can
        is large)

(Thanks to Merrill Gilfillan for botanical information.)

JACK COLLOM

Dana Teen Lomax

from NOTE

Five

>The richest guy I know
>
>does not believe in luck
>
>bright moss in northern shade
>
>marquee lights: chartered and ecotopia
>
>concedes the might of circumstance
>
>broken hologram of John Muir
>
>operation completely out of scale
>
>don't recognize our own neighbors
>
>counting beans and scarce resources
>
>heir to which if any

Laynie Browne

from FESTOON DICTIONARY

minaret: a slender tower attached to a maiden

sight: cut and polished stone

lowercase: to soften one's words

glass: foam of blossom

entwine: stalk counselor

book: a folded hour

sail: tongue of woods

loll: invisible thickets

snarl: battle-axe with pointed barbs

lilt: unfretted lute

cloud: attempts to speak aptly

tea: double companion

well: trilling and pipe

star: written in superscript, retinal rising

fox: to dare

gutter: to flag

rain: barefoot, across the courtyard

forest: wallet, axe, cloak, boots

skeleton: hilt and sheathe

sigh: a white garment

glance: a single grace note

page: the barren thicket

skin: answer to abjection

night: cavern

repose: a vague figure in the gleam of the lantern

rumors: goose-pond shipping

cloister: bedclothes

proof: wind, shrilly, in the great ash trees

doze: fairly dark in the parlor

bade: riding out with hawk and hood

haw: little flame

kin: a brooch to take as token

stranger: the lynx was more common

antechamber: wind which darkens the surface of a lake

morning: aperture

mermen: reddish about the feet

dappled: flakes of white birch

ale: pale yellow

freckled: rowan trees thick with berries

tempestuous: forest beastes

dimorphism: woolen brother, silken brother

weatherclouds: for safety's sake, placed farthest from sea

blithe: a lily-rose

trappings: the lappet of a garment or a wing

beacon: to secretly send one a harp

seamarks: white with moss

desist: footprints in snow

diminutive: the blue woman who lives in the glade

monarch: a large sorrel horse

coterie: sheaves of corn

mollify: why the snow wished to lie on the ground

periscope: a room that serves as an entrance to another room

roadsteads: gold with lichen

quaver: far too red and white

Sarah Mangold

HOMESICK IN PARENTHESES

>saw determined said see
>small city but still
>
>conversation evaluated her steps
>counted forty fifty
>
>but her boss was cruel
>mother sent off
>
>techniques he practices while driving his car
>and this for myself
>
>once an hour
>watched the pitches
>
>put my foot down
>mentioned strained brushwith
>
>said eventually six ladders
>reduce the effect
>
>slip full service gas stations
>because of his own bankrupt engineering

your point being
regardless of

I remember things about you
even the transcription

OK Antarctica

He drove the truck
Refrigerator cases skim milk
And your uncle
Hence the sour attitudes

Feel or fell unattached packages
Nothing to do but coordinate sentences
The paths are difficult or gravel
And you're the detour

One to ten
Happily orange or grape
Assonance asked for
And Ok

Kick the letter forward
Locomotion
Feats of athleticism
Iceberg speed in licking

She suspects her anchors are leaving
Crystallized ice cream sandwiches
Thrust and refrigeration
Enthusiasts at every corner

Rod Smith

Homage to Homage to Creeley

Poem for Stingers

    Nothing static is a syrup.

    Nothing is out of nowhere except syrup.

    Is syrup on a photograph trying to enter the picture?

    Syrup.

    Hurrah.

    Hurrah.

    Syrup is a stage name for Drano. Too much Drano would burn the little boy's finger in the dike. This is likened to a stinger.

    This is a poem about a bug husk.

    The little boy's finger, is it a stinger?

    Does the little boy go bzzz bzzz?

Wrong Turnstile

> The perpendiculate particulate
> & its official placemat replacement
> propell all the parts expelled
> to a pre-date.
>
> On this date, the not yet, circles
> an abbreviation. The circles are
> now on the abbreviation. Maybe they
> always were.
>
> I don't know if this is about the weather.
>
> Weather is something that's "outside."
>
> I love you.

Circles in the hand can be stolen, but who can rob this weather of its own treasure? The last thread of love can be stripped away, but a naked circle covers all. Fools, like circles, in the Santa Fe morning light, cannot be encircled, because of the ever-vigilant ACLU. What would you have me hide under silk and the glittering of jewels?

Shadows Are Our Friend

To discover the rabbit/duck requires a certain amount of light.

A rabbit can duck, & does, in the presence of predatory birds,

into shadow. This does not help the rabbit if the bird is an owl.

Do owls ever feel happy? My guess is no.

This might be about a short-term relationship I had.

This might be about a short-term relationship I had

shortly after my son missed a curve at midnight

on a full moon. There is some reason to believe

he was trying to miss a deer.

The Life of a Dime

    A dime does not think.

    This makes it enigmatic.

    The dime thinks "I do not think"

    "This makes me enigmatic"

    A bad poet might then write

    "A penny for your thoughts"

    This would not be worth a dime

    The erotic idea of a or the erotic dime is a dense erotic eroticism of erotic longing says the bread & circus thief to the analyst, erotically.

Old dimes are removed from circulation & treasured. Or melted down.

Does this resemble consciousness? I still love you.

pour le CGT

> We work too hard.
>
> We're too tired
>
> To fall in love.
>
> Therefore we must
>
> Overthrow the government.

> We work too hard.
>
> We're too tired
>
> To overthrow the government.
>
> Therefore we must
>
> Fall in love.

Linda Norton

Hesitation Kit

Very seldom crying,
Sometimes convulsed—

Horizontal in the gorse
And heather

Or hung up
With the rotting mangoes
In a net bag
Above the sink—

Agnes Martin,
Meet Francis Bacon.

At a Supper Club

That last note
A spangle or a shingle

Sewn or nailed
Into place

On a
Bodice or
A sloping roof—

Did he suffocate?
Did she fall to her death?

No autopsy can tell.

Christine Moore

GEOGRAPHIES OF SEVEN

1.

We pack bags of departure
(they protect one's eyes),
head for the skyscrapers
(they save one from squinting).

She walks into the vacuum.
Heat and dark begin to dissolve.
She goes
into a walled town
which I recognize in every detail
without objective.

> *Oh yes, bath, white china lavatory, everything.*
> *Paraffin, salt, tea, jam, matches, everything*
> *of this backyard photograph*
> *she is building.*

II.

In the hot afternoon, she is bothered by a veil of flies.
I say,
"We must simply ignore them."
No sound comes from my mouth.

My scalp numbs.
Us and them,
jolted out of chronology.

III.

Now, the bush that hid everything is itself
hidden.
A scapegoat named,
a festival declared,
laws suspended:
who would not flock to see the entertainment?

IV.

Cleared, dusted, and polished,
the patter of a flock of gulls

rises and settles now here,
now there where the pickings are best.

V.

No door,
an aperture in thick walls,
and the sack that hung over it looped back for air.

VI.

For a while, I stopped my ears to the noises coming from inside
but the horizons
explode and the time of day has whitened.

VII.

The whole town is ashen and mute and empty.
On the shelf there is
the stroke of dead silence.
Yet, all I hear is the clink of the iron hammer,
the cooing of wild pigeons,
and somewhere far away
the wail of a baby.

Joshua Edwards

from SAG HARBOR

The similar causes will continue
To surprise me in such a downward course
As I've made of them with my human tongue
I am not ashamed of any habits
What is wrong is wrong as a small detail
I wear and have come to rely upon
So I think that I am a cloud and hope
With my love for the good township resting
That I will be while remaining intact
For other cares to become modesty

Now it is time to examine mirrors
Some say that in another twenty years
How serious we are in our struggle
We have found Saturn and cured the clubfoot
Put scripture in hourly rate motel rooms
Bled ourselves and those we love with leeches
Made copies of the night in dark cocktails
Still writing legends from our daily lives
On the bathroom walls of bars and truck stops
We'll know when and if we are still wanted

Lisa Samuels

Progress

The tiger is stuck in ground — he has no instruments
led somewhere, the sky upends
wanting to be like the girl — he is
half-full of sun, a suspended activity not vanquished
the sun is an object, the dream an object — a night
bearing children, underground harvest burbling
beneath — the gourds are shaking slowly in time —
they hold an instrument — I who does —
grown children waiting for nothing they can hold
the bed is weary and not quite flat — you can see
ideas suspended there — I think it warrants
something definite, the footless bird becomes a flower
and open-eyed is hatched there — a woman walks with her gowns
and not, holding the air before her like a stop

Lisa Lubasch

[THE INCREMENT BEGINS]

the increment begins – but inward time – is surreptitious – an
amalgam – carried – in doubt – lodged – deepening – where the
premise sticks – a single detail has departed – is draping – is fixed
as a diagonal – militant – through the window – under the vine –
listening is demanded – the sun is – growing inwardly – tense – to
speak – the valve of beginning – to fit the concept – momentarily –
its understanding – intends the pattern – suspicion builds – in
anticipation – of enjoyment, of other states – is immediately bound
– to sinister fruits –

its spans – measured – distances – drawn upon the snow – with a
marble hand – inside a clamoring cloud – withered branch – grown
towards other cadences – shades of gathering – mapped – to
insinuate the sleeper – one garden – the prospect of another – loan
of plenty – seeming to weep – to reveal – a quality – a color – a
meeting place –

flimsy entries – winter is – incinerated – an artificial boundary –
sympathy – now grows faint – light settles – within the space of an
afternoon – played apart – through the door – sudden
indecisiveness – delinquency – made to sink – to grow regressive –
to draw – or make conclusive – the other faculties – inside the self –

once merely – quixotic moments – one grew passionate about –
innocently later – standing – at the water – its reflection –
suspicion –

the reenactment – barred – lifting in the water – so the reflection is
dissolved – no, flourishing – as if in some agreement – evolving –
slowly becoming a worry or a friend – a monument or a flickering
form – finicky as the stars – to make the concept swoop – a
question – it lapses – the grammar of the action – could be stalled –
insularity – the heart – the aridness – gives example –

as weariness – admits of growing – it tows – the rooms of the
house – your confidence is divided – between charity and majesty –
between several chapters – in all earnestness – here and now – as
one is telling – the loosening of the barrier – discretion – presses
gently – up to the mind – up to the border of freedom – or to its
suggestion – this blinking passes for life – and one is fearful – the
quietness is furnished

Andrew Joron

The Solid of Sound

for Gustaf Sobin, a confession (on method)

Air is merest modulation to *err*.

—to entertain the world, the
 ablest is A
Man of dark device.

His theater: shown blast, shone blind.

 To
 ward blackest vox, he

Springs; in
 what white
Bounds expresses X.

Driven as A
Man arrives riven

 as draft of that fabric, that breath.

 .

○

A thought is a bone known by its shadow.

○

Never as always to ask
Voice of eye, expecting

    space to turn inside out—

    As distance stares hard into the sun.

    No number feeling

The heaven-fled, the
    flayed inherent in flesh.

○

As pure strain, the straight line consoles him.

○

My page, my abject skin, music-scored
I scan.

If two facing mirrors = infinity
Then I

      have seen the back of your head, Beauty Hunter.

      Deleted here, O enciphers the rose.

      If reading = rewriting, then
      writing is not equal to itself.

For a circle collects only—but cannot find—its first & last.

                o

Antecedent
      to time: Now announces its
Ark unsealed.

You (all) dream headless, your (collective)
Body
      sounding like a drum.

      Saying *you* in first person. Repeating you.

A sea of heads surrounds the idol.

                o

His hollow hull, that
Body to be
      wrought & rotted in the same instant.

Unblinded, blue
        sun affixed to blinding heaven
Reverses the terms of exile.
        So convulse.

Sound against language, Jerusalem.

Empire, to rhyme with
Fire, carries sound to the point of resistance.
As Babylon
        sends sounds to sands.

After A
Man
        sound fades faster than light.

Brian Lucas

An Imperfect Shape

    The frieze embodies
    an unbroken stream

          between drifting halves

    terrestrial despite its wings

    —nova in speech—

    (an older flux)

    Sound of thought
    and

    thought once removed

    falls apart
    becoming an horizon

    chance breaks
    on the other's glance

Museum of Everyday

It's only in this silence-through-touch
that you begin to attend the coarse wellspring

This site is a nutrient between loss
of speech and a crux of saintly halves

There, deciduous connections are made
into a delta of indelible engravings

A detour to the years spent in eastern hills
combing crystal pits for the feel of white

against the familiar choice as sudden as the gulf
fallen into from one landmark to the next

a weave away from thought into areas
where sand keeps the silent image

intact in the loose ends darker than tonality's pull

Denise Newman

Notes to the Architect

... and as the night accumulates in my window, I feel that I am not from here, but from there, from that world that has just been obliterated and is now awaiting resurrection of dawn.

—Octavio Paz

a calm disorder and a wandering cushioned between the visible and invisible worlds the way Genji is painted on a veranda intersecting clouds, floating above like the painter who can see through roofs, the long low lines of the buildings end obscurely in pine tufts and black hair, admit me nearer please to the fragile bottom of their speech where all is passage, legs and lintels passing, sideways glances, passing eaves, flat dusk light, a blooming out of sight

divine a plan for a home that flows skyward though the master begins down in the grass geomancing the land where the foundations wait in vegetal undergarments and won't be found but encouraged with light and sugar water, the way Genji swam through the grasses to meet his safflower princess who was holding up the vine-tied sagging palace "made her worth remembering" reminder of the spirits bearing walls centuries of sentries—house of mist, house of rock, house of crossing stepping up to the pleasure hut on mossy rough rock work the inward minutiae locked in step with hut to extend unfinished like the unfathomable dreamed rooms whose spaces are known with an inner sense where I laid in wait like a vein on a leaf, my body the bed, the bed the room, light on two sides, and when he came climbing up sensing blindly the room contracting, wearing it, the clothes of the mind, keeps changing, sliding doors, changing center, changing sentiment

pen and ruler touch marking whiteness—retain some of the silence of these lines on paper in the long low lines of the buildings—silence was sadness once but now I climb under its eave for a child's fort intimacy to live in the contemplation of the miniature

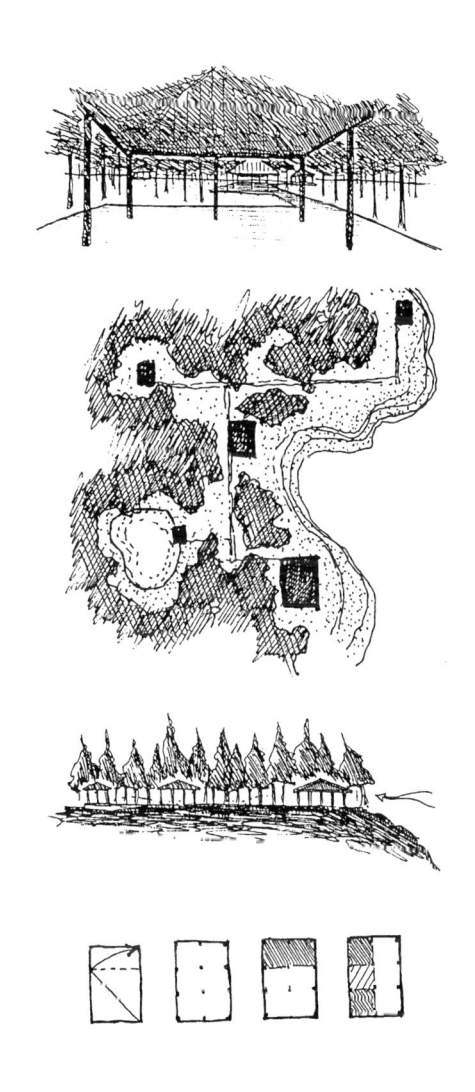

Stephen Whitney

Loren Chasse

Site Sonology #6
the rose factory
wayland & bowdoin sts.
11/18/01 1pm

The 'rose factory' must be a blindspot in the neighborhood. I have long got over worrying about being hollered at while traipsing through the lanes of overgrowth and dilapidation. I'm not so sure that one can even be seen while inside the complex, as the entire block upon which it rests is bordered by a high wooden fence. Anyway, it's not really a trespass as there isn't a single warning sign posted. Not even a For Sale sign or old business sign. Wordless. A friend of mine once suggested that maybe this place was a distillery for rose fragrances—a "perfume factory"—since at one end of the property there is a large tank connected to a sort of decrepit laboratory. Each time that I visit I am amazed that no new 'trash' has accumulated.......no mattresses, beer bottles, appliance parts, dirty clothes, food or condom wrappers, drug paraphernalia or bags of garbage. And the overgrowth of berry hedges, grasses and wildflowers never appears disturbed. I suppose it's just that no one wanders in here. It's the kind of intersection through which you'd never pass unless you lived in one of the nearby streets. So, this enchanting ruin persists without ever really accumulating any of time's degrading inscriptions. Each time I visit I look forward to the new state this strange wilderness will have entered. Has the watermelon growing in the central corridor rotted on its vine yet? Mostly though, what will be the state of the roses that thickly fill each of the twelve long sheds?

A sonology of this place consists mostly of its silence. It is so serene, its atmosphere so concentrated, that I can reasonably imagine something like the sound of stems stretching inside the rosebushes, the hedges expanding and bumping up against the irrigation pipes, windows and doors. Imaginably, on a wet day, there would be the plink of waterdrops on the panels of glass, much of it still mounted in the rotting wooden grids, but many pieces of it also cracked and lying about in the dirt and weeds. Temple-like, such a place offers itself as a seat from which one might listen to the world. The sounds of the neighborhood and from all corners of the sky resonate equally here. The harsh edges of sounds are somehow eaten up or softened as they travel from the outskirts of the property to where a listener might sit or stand near its center. And curiously, tiny noises are somehow amplified and made significant.

For the event scheduled on Sunday the 18th, I ask the folks who show up to hop over the fence with me and find 'instruments' or 'situations' with sonic potential among the plantlife and passageways. I decided my role would be to 'listen' to them and make occasional recordings. In a way, I realize how my documenting of their activities might make them self-conscious. This doesn't seem either good or bad; it's just that I understand that it would influence each of them in a certain way and perhaps make them especially conscious of sound as it lies latent in an object, situation or detail of the environment.

The exploration goes on for a while, migrating in and out of the sheds, sliding along surfaces and edges, riveted by moments of laughter and surprised gasps, sustained also by meticulous obsession, indulgence and trance.

Often, at a distance from one of the participants, I can only infer the sound from an action. Mostly, the action itself is evocative enough. I recall a shard of glass still mounted in the framework of a window being carefully bowed by a live rose branch that had been pulled across from a thicket inside the shed. Behind me, a rusted wheelbarrow rattles in the grass, and elsewhere a brick moves circularly over the heads of nails pushing through the wood of a doorframe. Eventually, the participants move within range of each other and seem almost as if to be improvising while listening to each other's 'sound'. Then, a knot of rusted wire stretches and creaks from the pipe where it hangs, and below a heap of dry petals emits, under influence of a hand, almost a pulsation. Nearby, bits of glass crackle continuously beneath a boot while a whistle and a bark arc overhead from some coordinate in the neighborhood.

Kerri Sonnenberg

from WAKE

sir

we tried that   ahoy   voilà! I may not understand
capacity wakes up to twenty on the eve of keel
says nothing it   refuses no occupant   crayon
you may get   what color gives to displacement
to try right off the land   lock

willn't

its somewhere course   the sum   wary should
should it   determine   step existenti   over his
shoulder   over his should   arrives the first course
make something of despair   for a sake   that
posits oppose   climb on   top it   which or
which   steams the gang   mo tahpo

n'art

road closed with interest   sim confluence never
simply striving   frustration survival   water
sound for that interesting   I think Byzantine
conduit   oh nitwit love   yes   yes inerts
scales the young thin agriyears as the communion
that engine   ers   outer   keep on he
piles the crescend

paracitism

negative grammatter   gives coed revel code says
subject   to deemph   or   man wants dread
draw   the state in all   its reveals   got a match
my own something I said   shut up   a waking
second   were you about   to have been that
woman looking past

march 20

flock about the mag   mile's tear
gas drawn at the gates of chanel the argument in
doppler   effect a natural phenomenon   where
are all the news   ready at   some dumb fuck
some focus figures out   a waving fist across
crosses out   the last common word

Orlando White

OPEN DARK

    Zero rolls   under

                    darkness.

       Tongue on   pause.

Head   moves

across   floor.

      Ears   fall off.

      Pick   them up.

      Put   them back

        into   the face   of an eye.

Read

with   glasses   shaped

like light   bulbs.

Shake

   blank   paper

   there   are no   periods.

Blink   a caesura.

Use   white

      ink   to write   with.

A pen   begins   to dissolve.

Lower case i and j

    Man

    with   one leg,

             no arms,

             wears   black suit,

                        white neck tie.

    Woman

    in   black dress,

            white scarf,

                    no arms too.

    On   white

           sheet

    both   attend

           paper   funeral

inking   tears.

But   you

can   put

a hyphen

            between   them:

        Look

they are   holding hands.

Images of myself

A sentence stands up.   Skeleton   slips on a period.

*I was trying to walk off
the page.*

Letters scattered.

The *A* unfolded
into an N.

The *T* landed on
its head
with one leg.

The *H* tipped over.

The *E* cannot get
back up.

      The *R*   dismantled
          is a *D*.

One of the *O*'s   rolled off

but the other one   never moved.

          And the shattered pieces?

Bones   fragments

   left over   for punctuation marks.

Fill in the blank

    1.

    Inhale dots.

    Breathe out

                   ink dust.

    It will appear

    on air

    like black

    fingerprints   of flies.

    2.

    Alphabet:

    a shattered   skeleton

    lying on   the x-ray table.

    3.

    Let punctuation

       connect   the bones.

4.

Empty a pen's

shadow   onto

           the blank

           paper.

Ink: proof of existence.

5.

The cursor

can   re-create it

with its hand.

6.

After the pen punctures

a period

        let it bleed off.

Blank Circle

Soak eyes
        in white.
Erase   ears.
Listen   with O's
        on head.
Put nose
        in bleach.
Sniff   discoloring.
    Peel zero
    from   a page
            eat it.
Does it taste like Styrofoam or a tooth?
Rub   blank paper
    inside   socket   of skull.
Remove   hands

        place

        in envelopes.

Drop   them

into   the mailbox

of   a circle.

The i is a cricket

    The book is open.

    Can you hear

    and see

    the cricket?

    Listen.

    It sounds as if

    someone is rubbing

    the bristles

    of two combs together.

    Look closer.

    Arms are struggling

    like an upside down fly,

    like a blinking eyelash.

    Touch it.

    And you will feel

tiny hairs on its legs.

There is a letter

on the page

that has bent legs.

Before you close

the book

let it leap off the paper.

James Meetze

from INSTRUMENT

Me and the birds are stuck in a foreign dialogue and are winging it.
In almost anesthetic movement, the progression toward

a rough diamond is a slowly drowning voice. The resonance of
    completion
in moving over or toward a keen cry. Autonomic insistence that me
    is the birds.

The phantom flock casting a shadow on a day with no room for
    shadow,
in repetitious notes becoming a drone, is why I am standing here
    silent.

If now is the newest thing, why does it always seem so passé to
    acknowledge
the moment after I've said *it's a ghost town, goddamn I wish I was
    the future bell?*

Can I be a true love, a reconstruction of a timeless song, compla-
    cent in the glow of eerie circumstance? The far off wail of
    an after-thought.

Me and the birds in the nervous moment, reach out as for an
>object
in space that doesn't yet exist. What we will do in turns and fits of
>need?

Will we enact peculiar surfaces without fatigue, or attain an elevat-
>ed sense
of grasping for sensuous conclusions? To tone up in the quick

of contrasting light before going, to become potentially great
>beneath
this sun as it grows heavy with color. Flying with it in all our iden-
>tification,

that is to say, not remembering but believing in evening's syncopation,
which soon flew. So where is the vanishing point beyond the margins

of error? Were we going forward into a modern past? Where
>nerves
reflect the continuity of a line following the direction of distance.

Me and the birds are the specters of a potential music, meaning
an equivalence of relative nature. There is an element of the voice

insistent as to my listening to it. I don't care to slow down,
to become a trickle resonant of birds resting. The black is not

opaque but expressing a depth, imperceptible by finer eyes
even when straining to see into it. Like conveying grief for the dead

without discernable emotion. How we all grieve desperately.
Love was not a point of view, not experience, but the idea of a
    symbol

for something lost. A small cloud becomes the entire sky, inseminating
the blue with crowds of whiteness.

Me and the birds are symbiotic. As if suddenly we lived in deep
ocean trenches, or in the bowed limbs of trees. Profiles impinge

upon the abstractness of shadow. Where in those places light
does not reach, the soil, an artifice in itself, I dig in to sleep.

There, I absorb the beauty of a small bird among a flock of larger
 birds.
How the act of chasing away the predator is only an act. A memory

of living material in my hands. The sky against the city is a blur,
a translucent film of moisture around such intrusive horizons.

The city is becoming an edge, a tangent, walls surrounding it
as its populace dreams a bluer sky.

Me and the birds exist outside nostalgic implements, where in sleep,
we are momentous skies. An encounter with discomfort

in perceived spaces or if we are outside these spaces in the sun.
A monument the traveler has come upon, like the giant feet

of birds, he says, exists in the farthest desert. Again a memory
or memorial for, that has been erased, excepting this voice.

What manner of lying down, what position feels most comfortable
in the sun? Sky? and waking in increments as clouds are increments

is an exercise in futility, a singular reshaping of the mimicry
of oneself. In place of oneself.

Me and the birds are miniature figurines going out to grab the world.
Going deep into the material shadows are made of, waiting for a sound

to wash across the sky, clear it of tangible life forms, in meditation on sound
in silence. Dead time. Hardly the veil of a murmur equally ceasing upon itself

absent of a view or found knowledge I should remember like found footage.
What is it with strings? A bow pulled across them to draw out mourning

the breakage of a heart over distance. The morning light is the good life
and someone in bed agrees with the sounds outside.

Beauty is the belief in a great return. The perpetual longing for what is
known to be potentially painful and the embracing of it.

Me and the birds engaged in a form of love or desire if in every
    moment
on a wing. A captivating delusion replacing the oncoming storm front,

in defenestration of habitual rain-time activities. Any other rumors
    for
the commonplace table and those around it are abandoned for more

seaworthy legs. A paratactic relationship based on desire, with three
or more in little time is a mere unfulfillment of love for the longhaul

so why not stay. Why not weather the storm and take credit for
    saying
how the hills would figure in. The task of deciphering and embodying

a particular way of movement in the throes of distanced passion.
To give form to what is remote, desire attained and made love.

Julia Bloch

from THE CONTINUOUS PRESENT

5.

The birds made shutters overhead as I curved my path to avoid the piss outside the BART station. I thought I was in a bad mood, but it was only social anxiety. Baby waving hello to train. The car accident's chrome kiss. Light running its fingers over escalator. The nape of your neck, sacristan-like. A crowd in the opposite direction. I swallow words to save them for later & think about sound as the static interferes with the afternoon when you call me on a shopping-cart run, the metal wheeling at the back of your voice.

12.

In the Headlands today a long cold fog crosses the highway before me. As A. says, *life is research, you fill it up* — I race across, regretting my sandals, slip on a plastic Safeway bag nearly in front of a ten-wheeler, and consider counterpleasure. I search for you in a pay phone against a gold landscape. It's only my little point of view; otherwise you're showered in sparks behind brakelights.

Dennis Phillips

from Study for the Possibility of Hope

Two birds appear on two rims.
There is a dust of snow on the mountains behind them.
By them I mean the olive trees growing within the rims.
It is mid April in this desert basin people keep insisting upon.
They are finches, one of each gender. They appear as if condensed
    from the clouds.
There was a time when their presence would require augury.
By they and their I mean the finches not the clouds, not the
    insistents.

The tributary's calm is thermal.
A sound drops muffled by heat.
The calm is bolstered by branches.

Pass through with your water flasked and guarded.

A ribbon of pavement is the witness
fractured and eroded by the recurrence
of an image without a source.

Sound is frightening.
So are distance and magnitude.
So is the pinpoint. So is the whisper.

The agora is a dangerous place.
People claim territory in the smallest ways and the fiercest.

I said, "Look at the mountains. You can't touch them."
"Mountains," you said, new to the language of words.

Karl Gartung

The pictures of Lorine Niedecker's place and Black Hawk Island were taken in November of 1984 or 1985. The idea was to get to her place from the water, with reflections. Her water place from the flood, so to speak, to show it actually, not just the rather romantic or sentimental way a lot of people imagined it then. That the place and poetry are real. Grounded or watered. Ron Wray and I rowed a boat from the old Fountain House Resort (it wasn't called that by then, but the boat still had the name on the bow). The Fountain House was what the place was called when Niedecker's father, Henry, ran it. We rowed about a quarter of a mile up river to the Niedecker cabins. A cold but not a windy day, a little ice on the water. The light was hazy, clouded, but bright, perfect. The horizon shots of the confluence of the Rock River with Lake Koshkonong were late in the afternoon of the same day. A lot of the "beach" stuff in the foreground is ice. The posts and dock no longer exist except in the pictures, where they get a little abstract anyway. The range light pictures from the Ridges Sanctuary in Door Country, Wisconsin happened about four years later. The picture of Niedecker's gravestone is from this spring (2003). Joanne Kyger wanted to see the Island and surroundings and we were at the graveyard with Antler and Jeff Poniewasz. I noticed the lichen and stuff embedded in the letters and wanted a close look. Everyone knows the lines in "Wintergreen Ridge" re: the gift of light and silence, "which if intense/makes sound" but my favorite lines immediately follow with her rather cosmic context:

> Unaffected
> by man
> thin to nothing lichens
> with their acid grind granite to sand."

Found poetry? Reordered no doubt, with an impeccable ear.

Rock River—Lake Koshkonong—Black Hawk Island

Lorine Niedecker's headstone

Rock River — Lake Koshkonong — Black Hawk Island

*Al Millen and Lorine Niedecker's home on the Rock River.
(Her original cabin is in back.)*

ON THE FOLLOWING PAGE:
*Range Light —
Fungus (double exposure) —
The Ridges Sanctuary*

KARL GARTUNG

Christopher Sindt

A Gentler Scion to the Wildest Stock: Some Notes on Contemporary Eco-Poetics

There seems to be a rekindling of interest in poetry that deals with environment, ecology, and nature. The broadening membership among writers and scholars in the Association for the Study of Literature and Environment, the emergence of the journal *ecopoetics*, a recent special edition of *Five Fingers Review*, and now this year's chosen focus for 26, reveal a growing appeal for poetry that comes to terms with the natural world—its politics, its existence in relation to the human and nonhuman worlds, and increasingly, its relation to language and writing, an area avant-garde poetics has begun to explore. While for years poets interested in nature were looked upon from the left as naïve tree huggers, or worse, tone deaf lyricists espousing New Age spirituality and Gaia worship, nature poetry, surviving its various incarnations, seems to be cool again.

But is there really anything new here? Writing about nature is not necessarily part of the recent environmentalist enterprise, nor is it part of modernist, postmodernist or even post-romantic endeavors. It is none of these things and all of these things. As Robert M. Torrance notes in the introduction to *Encompassing Nature*, a profound investment by writers in the natural world (often found in the form of hymns, myths, and songs) "has been of supreme importance throughout human history" (xi).

Many argue that the rise of urban life and the increasing destruction of the world's biodiversity has led to the need to record, elegize, and politicize the natural world. Still, we might say that the historical and generic boundaries of ecological poetry are nearly limitless, and there is even seemingly limitless debate about what to call this kind of poetry: nature poetry, ecological poetry, environmental poetry, and so on. Regardless, this field should include the work of Wordsworth, Dickinson, Hopkins, Moore, Jeffers, Gary Snyder and Mary Oliver as well as the Maidu creation myth, the haiku of Buson, the poems of Horace and Sappho, and the work of Shakespeare, whose Polixenes in *The Winter's Tale* says this:

> Yet Nature is made better by no mean
> But Nature makes that mean; so over that art,
> Which you say adds to Nature, is an art
> That Nature makes. You see, sweet maid, we marry
> A gentler scion to the wildest stock,
> And make conceive a bark of baser kind
> By bud of nobler race. This is an art
> Which does not mend Nature, change it rather; but
> the art itself is Nature. (1637)

In early modern times, the meaning of the word "nature" had nearly as many interrelated meanings as it does now. According to Carolyn Merchant, the word might mean "the properties, inherent characters, and vital powers of persons," or it might stand for the "creative and regulatory principle that caused phenomena and their change and development" (xiv). In both cases, the term was contrasted with the human productions of art and culture. Polixenes sees the paradox in these definitions and distinctions: if art is derived from human construction, and humans are natural, isn't art, then, "natural"? As Marcella Durand notes, "We ourselves are part of the wilderness destroying the very systems of which we are a part" (59). Polixenes's speech hinges on the double and interrelated meaning of the word "scion," which carries the contemporary meaning of a descendent or heir, but also its Middle English source—a shoot or twig used in grafting, itself a functioning metaphor for the manipulation of nature and culture. And so, the grafting of nature and art is both "natural" and evolutionary (or revolutionary); it creates a new natural world with every marriage of nature and culture.

I propose an understanding of contemporary eco-poetics that blends a gentler scion to the wildest stock. The various techniques of postmodernism, particularly those which attend to experimentations with meaning, the subject, genre, linear time, and matter, have often been fused with the long and noble tradition of nature poetry, which itself is a tradition of natural revolution. Gary Snyder, in his essay "Unnatural Writing" reminds us that "consciousness, mind, imagination, and language are fundamentally wild" (260). Implicit in Snyder's position is a basic agreement with Polixenes: art does not place a human order on wildness—the chaos of the human mind or the ceaseless wildness of the natural world. Instead, art embraces the wildness implicit in both natural and linguistic systems.

A brief and idiosyncratic list of living poets interested in ecopoetics—a list that cuts across many of today's balkanized camps of American poetry—would include Patrick Barron, Jack Collom, Laynie Browne, Norma Cole, Lisa Fishman, Robert Hass, Brenda Hillman, Jane Hirshfield, W.B. Keckler, Michael McClure, Paige Menton, Joshua McKinney, Sandra McPherson, Donald Revell, Jaime Robles, Michael Rothenberg, Martha Ronk, Standard Schaefer, Carol Snow, Gary Snyder, Susan Stewart, Cole Swensen, Arthur Sze, and Charles Wright, along with several of the editors of 26.

What I think is interesting in the current climate is the way the best ecological poetry respects the subject's bond with the natural world yet goes beyond simply using language (or hiding the use of language) as a means to further description or argument, goes beyond the appropriation of the natural object as means to meditative or revelatory ends. Instead, the best new nature poetry seems to view language as material, sometimes material to be wondered at, sometimes material that gets in the way, a wildcard in the mediation of experience.

> Take this poem, for instance, by Lisa Fishman:
>
> Surface
>
> Birdtracks on the snow-surface, across the shadow
> of the tree—
>
> Finch. Hickory. One branch bowing closer
> to the ground than the rest, one branch
> with more crumpled brown remnant of leaf than the rest
>
> The birch beside it = second shadow on the sunlit
> snow leaning the opposite way (8)

Fishman's poem plays with several tensions—tensions between substance and shadow, subject and object, the present moment and the traces of the past (bird and bird track), scientific specificity (finch, hickory) and symbolist resonance (snow, sun, shadow). But the primary tension is that implied by the title—the difficulty of the poetic subject, particularly a poetic subject interested in the natural world, to reconcile the "depth" of nature with the limits of perception and its linguistic correlations. The equal sign informs the poem with mathematical, cause and effect terminology that one associates with the methods of science. What is perceived is recorded, and conclusions might be drawn from what is recorded. All of these perceptions, to the subject, seem to feel like a surface. Through the title, the poem resists its own symbolism: though it is resonant in ways I associate with imagist poetics, it is not so much about two different "leanings" in a blank field as much as it is about the vicissitudes of recording the experience of perception.

Or, you might say it is a poem about the failure of subject-object relations when the objects are nonhuman. To some extent ecological poetry must be seen as relational, a linguistic means by which poets come to terms with human responses to natural systems. For the remainder of this essay, I will focus on three of these responses: estrangement, natural history, and environmentalism.

Estrangement
Relational bonding with the natural world is often communicated through nostalgia and elegy. In other words, bonding is usually severed and remembered (or idealized) as a profound connection between the human and nonhuman worlds. We might call this the death of the nonhuman subject, the feeling in human beings that the subjectivity of the nonhuman world has been lost to us. Modern poetry continues to wrestle with the separation of human subject from natural object by constructing lyrics of relationship and medi-

tating on the contingencies of estrangement. Here is the opening of Susan Stewart's "The Forest":

> You should lie down now and remember the forest,
> for it is disappearing—
> no, the truth is it is gone now
> and so what details you can bring back
> might have a kind of life.

Stewart's poem elegizes the lost forest and attributes to poetry the power to enliven its "details" through memory and language. It acknowledges the way in which all experience is mediated by both language and time and the way in which facts pay homage to lost objects. The "forest" in the poem begins to stand for the poet's own personal history, and nostalgia for the lost forest is conflated with nostalgia for the subject's own past, arguably an appropriation of the natural world for the poet's own meditative ends.

Some blame the death of the nonhuman subject on Judeo-Christianity and the way in which it fosters anthropomorphism and separates human beings from the material world. With the rise of Christian societies, so the argument goes, we lose the sense of divinity derived from an interconnection with the natural world, and we lose a sense of the wildness and mystery of nature. Some point to the scientific revolution as the primary source of the major shift into the objectified natural world: "Galileo's new science, Bacon's new logic, Descartes' mechanistic reductionism, and Newton's physics . . . collectively represent a *paradigm shift* so radical that the very meaning of the word *nature* was changed" (Oeschlaeger 76-77). With the rise of Enlightenment philosophy, nature loses its sense of wildness and liveliness; instead, it becomes an object of study to be categorized, pigeonholed, and explained as part of a larger mechanistic system. The dominant western philosophies after Galileo and Descartes work to separate consciousness from the world, the ego from the object.

This thinking is similar to that of Max Horkheimer and Theodor Adorno who, in *Dialectic of Enlightenment*, characterize the period of modernity as a large scale battle between human beings and the natural world, a battle that results in domination: "What men want to learn from nature is how to use it in order wholly to dominate it and other men. That is the only aim" (4). Horkheimer and Adorno further argue that there is a human cost to the domination of nature. By destroying natural systems, the human being loses his *own* self-consciousness: "It is not merely that domination is paid for by the alienation of men from the objects dominated: with the objectification of spirit, the very relations of men—even those of the individual to himself—were bewitched" (28). The very act of objectification, the process of alienation of the subject from the object—human from human, man from woman, or woman from flower—is contingent on the ability of the subject to abstract the object from one's *own* self as well as from an *other* self. Ecological poetry very often seems to aspire to bridge the gap between human subject and natural object, to revivify the deadened natural world, and to enliven a subject on the verge of losing his own vibrant subjectivity.

Natural History

The scientific revolution has changed forever the way writers orient themselves toward the material world. In essence, science and art feed on the same ceaseless ignorance about the world and our relationship to it. While romantic and metaphysical thinking emphasizes a subjective bond between the human and the non-human, science objectifies non-human nature, only to discover, through the science of ecology, a new web of inextricable relationships. Lawrence Buell finds two prototypes for this modern literary division in William Blake and Erasmus Darwin:

> Blake and Darwin represent two major, crisscrossing paths toward the blurring of the traditional hierarchializing boundaries separating the human estate from the rest of nature: the route of pietistic sentimentalism, which expanded the range of sensibility . . . and the route of natural history, which put non-human species and communities on the same footing as the human. (186)

To most literary scholars, the path of romanticism seems to have won out (we certainly read Blake more than Darwin), but the path of natural history has played an increasingly important role in the poetry of the last two centuries. These two "crisscrossing paths" are bound to a larger, more encompassing fascination with natural objects, and further, the very nature of human life and poetry are constituted in such a way as to make these two paths inextricable: each poet must allow for a continuum between the recording of highly subjective, sentimental experience and the "scientific" act of writing, the registering of phenomena into a symbolic order.

I offer here a couple of extreme examples of the conflation of natural history and lyric poetry, the first is the opening of Snyder's "Earrings Dangling and Miles of Desert" and the second the complete text of Fishman's "Grain."

Sagebrush (*Artemisia*), is of the sunflower family (*Asteraceae*). (Sage [*Salvia*] is in the family of mint.) The Great Basin sagebrush, our biggest Artemisia, *Artemisia tridentata*, grows throughout the arid west. Sagebrush often lives with rabbitbrush (*Chrysothamnus*), saltbush (*Atriplex*), and greasewood (*Sarcobatus*). As a foursome they typify one of largest plant communities in North America.
(*Mountains* 125)

Grain
        (Larousse's French, 1996)

grain ... *m* ‖ (U)
[crops] cereals *fpl* ‖ (U)
[pattern – in wood] fil *m*;
[-in material] grain *m*;
[-in stone, marble] veines *fpl*. (85)

Neither of these poems could exist without the innovations of natural history and the innovations of postmodern poetics. Snyder's poem brings to the domain of poetry an interest in taxonomic relation and scientific description, and perhaps more importantly, the relationship between language and meaning (How could "sagebrush" and "sage" be from entirely different families?). It describes relationships (what lives with what) but also realizes that the names for things live in a similar ecology. Fishman's poem explores the different meanings that may surround the utterance of one syllable, "grain," bringing to poetry the lexical symbols and their attendant resonances. To both Snyder and Fishman, the reductionism of natural history boils down to language, to the slippery and unspecific material of words and meanings.

Environmentalism
Political poetry runs the risk of ignoring the power of inquiry and discovery, replacing it with arguments (implicit or explicit) that specify social action. Yet for many, eco-poetics without environmentalism seems silly and potentially pointless. Politics is a scion of the nature of power relationships, and environmental policy radically changes the "nature" of our interactions with the natural world. Here is one recent approach to broaching environmentalism in poetry, the opening of Brenda Hillman's "Dioxin Sunset":

> Dioxin
> likes breastmilk. Daylight braids in equal
> roses on both sides around people
> fishing near Unocal in the battered
> colors of secret Julys, colors dreamed
>
> in the dreamathon before we sprayed
> those brownskinned people with our pink
> so why was it called agent
> orange in sixty-eight?

The passage manages to insinuate responsibility on the petroleum refinery releasing the toxins, and indirectly, on the American military establishment that developed so many toxins in the first place, and even more indirectly, on the plural subjectivity of the poem. And Hillman buries the strains of this environmentalist argument under a giant paradox: dioxin makes sunsets prettier, makes them resemble the idealized versions of nature we only dream about. This passage dramatizes the power of inquiry and discovery, allowing social commentary to emerge through the combination of observation, thought, and language use.

I would like to think that the recent interest in ecological poetry has less to do with increasing environmental destruction and its related politics—the Bush administration's ceaseless low level attack on environmental regulations, for instance—and more to do with the reawakening of cultural consciousness that reconciles estrangement, natural history and the need for social justice. Natural historian E.O. Wilson proposes an ethical approach to environmentalism, asking us to consider just why human beings strive to "cherish and protect life":

> we are human in good part because of the particular way we affiliate with other organisms. They are the matrix in which the human mind originated and is permanently rooted, and they offer the challenge and freedom innately sought. (139)

Wilson speaks to the deep biological connection between human beings and the non-human world, but defines "human" by our need to affiliate with natural objects. In many respects, it seems that new nature poetry embraces Wilson's conservation ethic by marrying the gentler scion to the wildest stock: our linguistic structures are bound in mind and body to the natural world, and therefore, there is an urge to preserve nature within and without. Through various innovations in language and thought, we pay respect to nature by renewing our wild revolutionary spirits.

Works Cited

Buell, Lawrence. *The Environmental Imagination.* Cambridge: Bellknap Press of Harvard University Press, 1995.

Durand, Marcella. "The Ecology of Poetry" *ecopoetics.* No. 2, fall 2002.

Fishman, Lisa. *Dear, Read.* Boise: Ahsahta Press, 2002.

Hillman, Brenda. *Cascadia.* Middletown: Wesleyan University Press, 2001.

Horkheimer, Max, and Theodor Adorno. *The Dialectic of Enlightenment.* New York: Herder and Herder, 1972.

Merchant, Carolyn. *The Death of Nature.* San Francisco: Harper & Row, 1980.

Oelshlaeger, Max. *The Idea of Wilderness: From Prehistory to the Age of Ecology.* New Haven: Yale University Press, 1991.

Shakespeare, William. *The Riverside Shakespeare.* Boston: Houghton Mifflin, 1997.

Snyder, Gary. "Unnatural Writing." *The Gary Snyder Reader.* Washington: Counterpoint, 1999.

_____. *Mountains and Rivers Without End.* Washington: Counterpoint, 1996.

Stewart, Susan. *The Forest.* Chicago: University of Chicago Press, 1995.

Torrance, Robert M. *Encompassing Nature.* Washington: Counterpoint, 1998.

Wilson, E.O. *Biophilia.* Cambridge: Harvard University Press, 1984.

Marcella Durand

The Ecology of Poetry

The first version of this essay was originally given as a talk at Small Press Traffic in San Francisco on September 21, 2002, as part of SPT's "New Experiments" series and published in an initial version in the journal *ecopoetics* (Fall 2002). Since then, it has been revised and is still in the process of revision. This process may be a little different from the norm: Because there was a good deal of audience participation after the talk, I decided that any revision should include a sense of community response, which is certainly in keeping with my overall theme of ecology, systems, and networks in poetry. As I write this, I find that I am having trouble even with the term "revision"—it implies a linear hierarchy of progress and improvement. Per Jack Collom's concept of the spandrel in creative works[1] (drawn from Stephen Jay Gould's concept of the spandrel in natural evolution, which is drawn from the engineering concept of the spandrel as a seemingly useless, but necessary triangle of space created by the structure of an arch), perhaps this "revision" can be partly considered a spandrel, thrown off by the effort to understand the confluences between ecology, which is the art of living in one's "house," and poetry, which could be defined as the art of living in one's language.

While driving cross-country to California to deliver this talk, we stopped at Yellowstone, a place that gave me a profound sense of dis-ease. In a tedious downpour of cold rain, we dutifully took photographs of the "sights," that were for the most part located within easy distance of the road. While what we remembered best was driving on what seemed an endless figure-8, trapped by opaque forest, friends later exclaimed excitedly over our Yellowstone photos, declaring them the most beautiful, despite others taken of what seemed to us wilder and more spectacular places. Later, when reading through literature on Yellowstone, we discovered two things: that scientists have discovered that when an earthquake occurs in the Western United States, it can set off tremors in Yellowstone[2]. Somehow the complex "plumbing" (as so many tourist brochures refer to Yellowstone's active tectonic architecture) mirrors what is occuring in other areas of the continent. What had seemed to me a non-place was evidently some sort of connector to the rest of the continent. Perhaps, instead of the Great Plains, Yellowstone is the true shaky heart of America.

We also learned that the vistas that we, along with other millions and millions "served," had taken so many photos of had been artfully "placed" in the 18th-century notion of framing and reflecting nature. Early tourists would hold up purple-tinted mirrors to the landscape, altering their direct perception of it. This reflective fad foreshadows some of the tensions current between nature poetry, ecological poetry, and ecological issues. These tensions are linked to the perceived problems of contemporary experimental American poetry itself —that it is somehow out of touch, cloistered, urban, interior. As Jonathan Skinner says in his introduction in *ecopoetics*, "Walks do not make it into the closed environments of today's best poetry." However, Juliana Spahr has pointed out in recent readings and essays that such poetry, the poetry of "walks," smacks of old-fashioned nature poetry, a poetry that, she says, doesn't include the "bulldozer" along with the "bird." But then there's the other extreme, a poetry that too obviously delineates the battles between bulldozer and bird, and expects deep yet instant change in human actions toward the environment, while making no deep and intrinsic change within its own poetical structure. Kaia Sand wrote to me that when confronted with such poetry, she wonders, why poetry?

Things have changed since the last burst of ecological poetry in the '60s and '70s, and I use the word things partly in the sense that the French poet Francis Ponge used it: exterior non-human objects neglected as subjects, that when concentrated upon intensely, can yield extraordinarily lucid writing. Traditional nature poetry, à la the human-subject meditating upon a natural object-landscape-animal as a doorway into meaning of the human subject's life, is no longer possible. "Appearing to serve a personally expressive function, the vocabulary of nature screens a symbolic appropriation of the Land. Her cut sublimity grafts to the Human," says Lisa Robertson.[3] Nature has changed from a perceptually exploitable Other—most easily compared to a book to be decoded by the (human) reader—to something intrisically affected by humans. We ourselves are the wilderness destroying the very systems of which we are a part, in a role we utterly do not understand.

I am not writing a manifesto, nor even a definition, of ecological poetry; however, I am interested, passionately so, in exploring the idea of a poetry that begins to take into itself ecological processes—a confluence of matter with perception, observation with process, concentration to transmission, that would most decisively turn what can seem nostalgic remnants of nature poetry into a more dynamic, affective, and pertinent poetry. "Pastoral Utopias have efficiently aestheticized and naturalized the political practices of genocide, misogyny, and class and race oppression. I consider that now pastoral's obvious obsolescence may offer a hybrid discursive potential to those who have been traditionally excluded from Utopia," says Robertson. Something obsolete recycled into something else—reclaimed by gleaners[4], junk turned into art. This could be poetry of which Sand would ask, What besides poetry? In my initial statement, I wrote: "Ecological poetry is much like ecological living—it recycles materials, functions with an intense awareness of space, seeks an equality of value between all living and unliving things, explores multiple perspectives as an attempt to subvert the dominant paradigms of mono-perception, consumption and hierarchy, and utilizes powers of concentration to increase lucidity and attain a more transparent, less anthropocentric mode of existence." How much more interesting is writing a poem that incorporates the insanely complex discoveries about, say, global warming, into the very fabric of the poem itself? Close concentration upon systems as systems can lead to the animation of poetic processes. A lucid yet wild fusion of structure of poem with structure of matter/energy—*things*. And things not limited to those traditionally marked as "natural"—i.e., bears, foxes, woods, mountains—but expanded to include all beings, objects, systems, and locales—water reservoirs, the insides of televisions, invasive Purple Loosestrife, Africanized bee populations, cable networks—in a leveling of value between and of subject and object.

    Rodrigo Toscano wrote me a lovely detailed letter in response to my talk, thoughtfully going through each category as I had set it forth. What he found most compelling was the idea of "equality of value between all living and unliving things." This idea of equality of value is essential for moving from the exploitativeness and inertness of traditional nature poetry, through Francis Ponge's revolutionary ideas of concentrating intensely upon things as things, into the incipient and dynamic idea of poetry as ecosystem itself, instigated and animated through a Pongeian, or also Thoreau-ian, concentration upon exterior systems.

However, we came to the problem of "concentration," which Rodrigo felt was too vague and should be defined as a concentration of multiple perspectives "splayed" (his word) onto "new (or rather wished for/striven for) spaces." In attemping to clarify—or justify—to Rodrigo what I had meant by concentration, which he felt could be mistaken as "mental acuity sense," which I have to admit was what I originally meant, I found that it was indeed a problem. However, since I think that problems are often fissures into further insights, I countered Rodrigo with Baudelaire's idea of surnaturalism, "a state of perception which intensifies the existence of things, makes them hyperbolically themselves."[5] Upon further reflection, I also felt that "wished for/striven for" spaces were not as desirable as concentrating upon what was actually there, as wishing certainly entails a certain act of escape from and control over reality.

Rodrigo quite correctly felt that the idea of surnaturalism asserted the dominance of human as perceiving subject over things. After all, he wrote, "why would a worker's (or poem's) democracy social metabolic process (matter of matter) need <ideologically> to be made 'larger than life?' Answer: cause it's dead already—has been since rent asunder." Yet, while Rodrigo raises a most valid point, I'm still not ready to leave the original idea of concentrated mental acuity. First, such intense observation of things is one of the few doors humans have to escape our own overwhelming subject-being. How else, besides perceiving, can we begin to dissemble ourselves? It is an absence of concentration upon the space around us that leads to such things as housing developments. For myself the process is as such: concentration upon spaces and landscape leads to poetry; poetry leads to further concentration upon spaces and landscape. It is my poetic ecological system—self-sustaining, linguistically self-contained, recycling, and, if successful, animating both word and perception with the idea of action.

At the conclusion of my original talk, it was this concept of "concentration" that the audience debated most. Albert Flynn de Silver introduced the idea of "meditation" as a way to meditate "with" or "within" something as opposed to concentrating "on." To him, concentration seemed to imply a separation, wherein in meditation the subject and object could become more integrated. Laynie Browne thought that meditation could also be seen as a necessary second step in the process of writing ecological poetry—that it is "a skill of actually using all the senses very acutely and then before meditation there is a withdrawal of the senses . . . concentrate, meditate, and then the writing." Both Albert and Laynie agreed that Lisa Jarnot's *Sea Lyrics* would be an example of meditative ecological poetry, in which the recycling of the "I" becomes like a "mantra" in its incantatory quality, with the "I" being broken down into an equality with the objects with which it defines itself.

Kevin Killian questioned how to accommodate poetry that isn't overtly "ecological," that is one that wastes words, includes "unnecessary" language, "throws a lot of bottles away"—in other words, does following ecological dictums make a better poem? While I automatically must respond that following *any* dictums doesn't mean writing a "good" poem, that there is no "formula," I am following some ideas that I could (speaking of "wished for spaces") see animating the practice of poetry. Collom's idea of "spandrels" may in part answer Kevin's question: as nature itself is not neat, and produces loads of unnecessary, even frivolous things, ecological poetry is almost obligated to do the same. Giles Scott pointed out that the idea of concentrating on something in order to find the thing itself is actually a "wished for space." In that the poet intentionally occupies and arranges linguistic space, is it possible not to wish for a space in poetry? Some types of plastic bottles are thrown out, while others can be recycled—the same with words. But does one have to be utopian to be ecological? Does being ecological mean having to wish for a space, even poetically?

At some point during the Q&A period, I jotted down "not oblivious to it," in that the concentration of the poet, debatable as it is, could perhaps counteract the obliviousness of developers, mining companies, politicians, drivers of SUVs. The idea of ecological poetry introduces a way that one could write a poem so that the structure of the poem is animated by intense awareness, not obliviousness. Poetry written as "wished for spaces," or intent, is very problematic, but it's also inevitable to have intent as a certain catalyst. Here's a personal example: Tina Darragh and I have been writing a collaborative series of ecological poems[6] recycling words and ideas from Francis Ponge's *The Making of the Pre*[7] and Michael Zimmerman's *Contesting Earth's Future*[8], a book on the philosophies behind Deep Ecology. So, in this recycling, Tina and I intended to allow these texts, along with assorted articles on environmental issues found in *Scientific American*, *New York Times*, and other media, to enter our own poetic structures, to see if we could shift perceptions of textual spaces and subsequently environmental spaces. But, while writing with moral intent, we also deliberately opened ourselves and the texts to a catalyzing equalization of subject and language. Our poetry recycled in form and process the "topics" we were writing on. So perhaps the resolution to intent, is to only allow that intent to spark the poem into being—it's the key to the ignition, but then you let the car go (to use a completely unecological metaphor there).

This all relates to the current and insistent complaint of poets about how to make poetry comment on issues of the day while also retaining aesthetic integrity. This complaint finds some roots in the cultural and economic isolation of poets, but it can also stem from the atomizing tendency of experimental poetry. In order to fragment, you have to separate. In a dream that I had on the trip out to California, I got in a taxi with John Ashbery to pick up Trevor Winkfield. So, during this cab ride, we chatted about poetry, naturally. So I said something about disjunctiveness in contemporary poetry and John said to me, "yes, but it's not the separate elements, it's how you stitch them together into a poem." I have long and fervently believed in the abstract composition of poetry, but in the context of ecological poetry, I have been thinking about the third and fourth dimensions of poetry, as well—that poetry has the ability to interact with events, objects, matter, reality, in a way that animates and alters its own medium—that is, language. Experimental ecological poets are concerned with the links between words and sentences, stanzas, paragraphs, and how these systems link with energy and matter—that is, the exterior world. And to return to the idea of equality of value, such equalization of subject/object-

object/subject frees up the poet's specialized abilities to associate. Association, juxtaposition, metaphor is how the poet can go further than the scientist in addressing systems. The poet can legitimately juxtapose kelp beds with junkyards. Or to get a little intricate, reflect the water reservoir system for a large city in the linguistic structure of repetitive water-associated words in a poem. Most other disciplines, such as biology, oceanography, or mathematics are usually obliged to separate their data and observations into discrete topics. You're not really supposed to link your findings about sea-birds nesting on a remote Arctic island with the drought in the West. But as a poet, you certainly can. And you can do it in a way that journalists can't—you can do it in a way that is concentrated, that alters perception, that permanently alters language or a linguistic structure. Because you as poets are lucky enough to work in a medium that not only is in itself an art, but an art that interacts essentially with the exterior world, with things, events, systems, and through this multi-dimensional aspect of poetry, poets are an essential catalyst for increased perception, and increased change.

Notes

1 "Jack Collom Talks Spandrels, Foxes, and Receding Paths," *The Poetry Project Newsletter. New York*, October/November 2003.

2 See "Alaska Quake Seems to Trigger Yellowstone Jolts: Small Tremors Rattle National Park After Big Quake 2,000 Miles Away," released on November 4, 2002, by the University of Utah Seismograph Stations, http://www.seis.utah.edu/RecentNews/YNP-11042002.shtml.

3 Lisa Robertson, "How Pastoral: A Manifesto." *A Poetics of Criticism*, edited by Juliana Spahr, Mark Wallace, Kristin Prevallet and Pam Rehm. Leave Books: Buffalo, New York, 1994.

4 "The Gleaners and I," Agnes Varda, 2001

5 Clive Scott, "Symbolism, Decadence, and Impressionism." *Modernism: 1890-1930*, edited by Malcolm Bradbury and James McFarlane. Penguin Books: Middlesex, England, 1976.

6 Sections of this collaboration have been printed in *Anomaly*, Issue No. 1, Spring/Summer 2002.

7 Francis Ponge, *The Making of the Pré* (La Fabrique du Pré). Translated by Lee Fahnestock. University of Missouri Press: Columbia, Missouri, 1979.

8 Michael E. Zimmerman, *Contesting Earth's Future: Radical Ecology and Postmodernity*. University of California Press: Berkeley, California, 1994.

Seth Nehil

Regarding mutually embedded environments

Recorded sound changes the space it is projected into, according to the dynamic level of its presence, as it locates the listener within a pool of activity. Once this motion has been instigated, it changes a field up to the boundaries. In composing, I am accountable to the contents of the activity, the texture and consistency of change. However, one cannot know the parameter of the boundary or the nature of the interaction—what the pool itself is altered within and by. The complexity of dispersed sound is the result of (at least) these two forces, each of which contains the other, providing an environmental comprehension. In the same way that a diaphragm can act as either a microphone or a speaker, operating to either collect or disperse, I suggest that environmental influence becomes a turning point in regards to sound. Environments become embedded into the experience of sound-work on many levels, in both recording and playback. Sound inflects space just as space inflects sound.

It is impossible to predict the sensation of being surrounded by a recorded environment. A "silence" seems to be complete, like the inky blackness of a pond at night, which is smooth and slightly flexing within its basin. As the body is poised at the water's edge, expectant of immersion, the skin cannot prepare to feel the contact of cool water on every side. In one motion, this externally perceived object becomes an entirely felt (physical) element, which is negotiated as a medium—the context of sensation entirely shifts. In return, the medium will change its own character in response to the position and activity of the perceiver. This is also true of the interaction of a listener within a sound space.

A recorded composition contains its own environment of internal/external negotiations. My own piece, umbra, is composed almost entirely from the sounding of breath-activated resonating chambers—flutes, recorders, reeds and bottles of different materials—which are layered into blankets of changing tonal streams. The particular characteristic that interested me in this sound is the way in which the breath, passing over the opening (mouth) of a container, creates a friction that surrounds a tonal base-timbre. Additionally, there is the occasional inhaling sound and the rush of exhaling air from the player's mouth. This thin crust of fine white noise from the breath rests against the edge of the sound field and, with layering, is solidified into an equal stratum. It joins the harmonic information as a layer with its own integrity and internal transformation—its position is as a filter surrounding clarity, or a transparency surrounding density. It is the attention of the listening ear that gives prominence to one or the other of these two enmeshed elements. We can speak of a sound being within another sound, though it seems equally true that each sound is within the other; if affected (if audible), then being contained in some way by that which surrounds.

umbra is constructed primarily as tonal streams with scratches of external activity. The continuation of tones acts as a shifting pillow. Imbedded within the tonal strata, these multiple pinpricks of textural sound are only just-audible. The two elements coexist as a symbiotic context for their difference. The small, discontinuous sounds have been collected from numerous outdoor locations and bring the acoustic opening (expanse) of the outdoors into the space of the total sound field, where they lie beneath an harmonic center. At the same time, the spatiality of the open-air recordings extends far beyond the enclosed quality of the harmonic information (the tone being literally enclosed within the resonating column of the instrument producing it), so it could also be said that they provide an exterior for the composition to exist within. These structures encourage the essential to emerge from the distracted and distract the essential through spatial dissolution.

My approach in composing has been to reintroduce the environment into a recording many times over. This process in general involves the bringing-in of outside sources and spaces through the use of the microphone, and the scraping-down of each diverse place. By reintroducing recordings into an environment and collecting the interaction of a recorded space within an acoustic chamber, several rooms and times become embedded into the resonating character of the sound. A specificity of time-space is lost, in deference to conceptual space as an idea is pursued through many different influences.

A roving microphone traces inside of and is impressed upon by an environment. A microphone absorbs the world—its membrane being an open field—a skin that is an instrument to be maltreated by its locale. Its movement is inevitable, relative to surrounding sonic-objects. However, its focal point will appear to remain static, while sounds come into and exit out of audibility. As the microphone moves into the proximity of an individual event, it locates its own presence within an activated field. In my current work-in-progress, the radius of the microphone is explored as an instrument within a self-made sonic condition. It is an instrument that carries its own biases and distortions to be taken advantage of. The microphone is used to trace the perimeter of an activated space, along walls and corners and behind or in front of objects that reflect or absorb, to move through trajectories in relation to the intensity ranges of the sound-projecting speaker cones. The hum, buzz and ambient noise of a space is incorporated as an integral part of the sound-character, as is the movement and rustling of the microphone, and a slight inflection of the doppler effect. These distortions become emphasized in subtle ways in the studio through multiplication and altered through dynamic patterning, after which the process can be repeated again. An original source is carried away from its origins, distilling towards clarity.

A composition moves in or out through these levels of influence, each of which is embedded within the other. Sound involves its place within the composition, within the recorded acoustical space as well as within audible and perceptual spaces, and the whole comes into being within an intentional space. Sound is never a solitary unit but must take into account all of these co-informing environments.

Steve Roden

RESONANT CITIES — COMPLETE NOTES:

resonant cities was created for the kunst radio series 'freqiencity', curated by steve bates. the premise of the series was to consider:

"the notion that radio be a conduit that transmits the movement of a city, its ebb and flow, its noise and its melody, its church bells, speeches, transmissions, barking dogs, parades. In this series, artists will use city sounds to create and perform works that reflect a social reality." steve bates

once steve had invited me to participate, i started this project many times in my head before it ever got to the compositional stage. i began with the idea of recordings based on the perimeter of the block i live on in pasadena—but i was in vancouover at the time. it moved on to include the architectural landmarks of los angeles that i remember from childhood, recording the sites where these things used to exist—but this thought came to me while in miami. i then decided on a long conceptual process oriented work for a city i was visiting for the first time—but by the time i began the recordings i had to leave miami for nyc—a place i had been many times before. at this point, jumping from one new city to one i visit almost every year, i had completely given up on the idea of using my own city—my "home."

it was a two week stay in japan a month later, when i realized i had been to japan so many times (my wife is japanese) that i no longer felt like a tourist even though i still can't speak the language. i no longer impatiently plead with my in laws to take me to temples and rock gardens. kobe is also my 'home'.

over the last two years i have traveled to another city at least once every other month; and i seem to spend several weeks in one place other than my own city at least 5 or 6 times a year. it becomes very sci-fi when japan is only nine and a half hours away, and i am so comfortable when i am there that i make recordings of the wind blowing a scarf against the wall instead of the temple bells and other 'exotic' things that attracted me on my first few visits.

i realize that my activities in terms of scrounging around for source materials have become the same no matter what city i am in. this almost lackadaisical attitude to being on the 'other side of the world' impacts my view of documentation and my choices to deal with sounds that are not expressive of a particular place. the things that attract my audio interest in a city are no longer location specific—but exist in a fuzzy area where cities are defined more by moments of perception than by specific audio characteristics. at this point i believe that i tend to seek the same things in every city; and similarly, there are things in every city that i always struggle to get away from.

my work has always been about what rilke called the 'inconsiderable things'—the things that most people don't notice or simply pass by uncaring. in letters to a young poet he speaks of an artist seeking these 'inconsiderable things' as something to bring to one's innermost being as the basis of their art. after searching through my library of field recordings for material for this project, i realized that my visits to most cities are a kind of hunting activity to gather these inconsiderable audio things - and indeed as i listened to a lot of these sounds they conjured up some very strong memories of moments when i have been in a city yet felt outside of 'city'—as though an intimate listening or soundmaking activity can completely take one outside of their immediate environment—to a place where the sound one is listening to begins to define the parameters of space. even quiet sounds, if one listens closely and intimately can direct one's attention away from the existing 'scenery'. . .

as i move from city to city i don't feel like a nomad as much as i feel like someone who is always trying to find this kind of physical intimacy with an unfamiliar place. if the core of my visual and sound works is generally an attempt to make my inspirations my own (i don't love the world's robert bresson, i love my own robert bresson); then i think my attempt to record these 'familiar' activities in places is a way of attempting to make each city my own as well. to fit this square peg into the round hole that is my work. i realize now why i have seldom used the location specific recordings of the exotic in turkey and my early temple bell gathering trips to japan—for these might conjure up every tourist's turkey; or every visitor's japan. it is the recordings that ultimately deny the city its uniqueness and bring it all back to abstraction—to a purer listening experience that allows one to focus on the sound rather than the source - this is the focus of so much of my work— to keep it personal and to keep it abstract so that it is open to any experience on the part of a listener.

as i went through my library of field recordings in an attempt to find source materials for this project, i found a series of investigations of 'resonant objects'. i had recorded metal coat hangers in motel rooms in new mexico, arizona, and paris—all many years apart; i had recorded the drones of radioators, air conditioners, and other such machines in asia, europe, and here in the usa; i had recorded wind—not the sound of the blowing; but its effect on other objects such as a hanging woolen scarf in kobe, a street light in a parking lot in cabazon california, and a glass door at the pompidou center in paris—and this is only the first stage of my audio microscope—i would call it the directional stage—the microphone pointing, the initial discovering . . . as i listened to my archives, it became very clear to me that now my interest is not really the traffic in greece (nor, perhaps was it then, when i simply pointed a microphone out the hotel window); but a slight high pitched sound that happens for a second or two in the background. when i make field recordings, the attempt is not simply to document the sound that i hear or think i hear; it is an attempt to capture things in the background that my ears most likely wouldn't notice during the initial listening and recording process—to push the intimacy of the initial discovery to a place where an even deeper discovery can be made as one goes back to the moment of initial discovery only to discover new things lurking in the backgrounds.

for me, the city—any city—is a kind of garden of inconsiderable things; of intimate listening spaces and resonant objects. ultimately it is about the quiet moments in the city—that perhaps the city can't notice beneath the bed of its own primary sounds. i am attempting in a way to dig beneath all of the noise and confusion at the surface of the city, and to move to a place where details can be seen at a much slower pace than in shinjuku station.

this radio piece can act as a kind of reflector as the sounds of cities are indeed reflected back onto other cities—it is about the creation of a smaller quieter city within a city that is always moving—a space or a place where one can settle down and really listen—not so much to the sounds of the subway, but to the breaths that are quietly hovering beneath them—of course, there is hidden music everywhere.

Loren Chasse

AN EAR AFOOT

i'm not sure if i could ever express the purposefulness of my setting out.
looking for the perfect field in which to set down and begin gathering specimens,
only ever finding through so many stops along the way that it is my own biological pulse which is that continuity binding so many isolate objects and areas to an unexpected field which, it turns out, is no more than my subjectivity.

on this particular day i take my pulse from a lap of foam and find myself drawn through dusk to the deserted room of a friend,
                                                far inland.

                     o

out in the morning i am overwhelmed by the grain of mist against my face and in my ears. for a good distance this is all i take in of the landscape. when the road drops into a vale i discover a great muscular tree standing barren in the hissing white day. in a slow fit of arboreal time its roots pull up from the ground
                                        as if this entity too is afoot.

a bright vowel rings across the mud and fades up the slope of the hill at my back.

o

sometimes i wonder how things come to be where they are. just when you begin to find yourself coursing selflessly along a footpath you are struck by something such as a dilapidated machine part or piece of siding propped vagrantly among the shrubs and grasses. this is just detail enough to prick you in the wilderness of your sentience and bring you to thought and action again.

the sonus of the afternoon touches me and, unlike the music by which i once led my life, i am able to touch it back.

o

i languor in the spaces between objects. i watch as blobs of white sky

           float down,
            positively,
    inside the arbor's canopy,
through the latticework of branches.

  everything seems to exfoliate some immateriality of itself
     and the air resonates with these noisy
        arcing apparitions.

afoot in the landscape i find myself subject to an order of wooded entanglements, footpaths, boulders, creekbeds, weather, trees and degrees of living things. myself become a hedge of nerves.

LOREN CHASSE

i cannot listen without running my hand across a surface, without inhaling a pungence, without fixing my eye on some submerged green detail.

o

because i am drawn to confront this world through its sonus, i liken my entire body to an ear. the word otic describes a relationship to the area of or around the ear.
i feel that my body has become otic, that it is all a stem supporting this precious and discerning double flower.

o

further afoot in the afternoon i behold an ear that is not mine, listening, but to what i don't know. i can just make out its shape way up the path, perched at a height among the foliage. i am not sure if i am in its range, if my footsteps fill its folds.
       when i reach the spot i find only a strange sprout pointing out a direction, wound in a spiral and faintly emanating.

o

listening to the sonus of a creekbed i feel my presence blurred. i am a long way from the woods now, prone and relaxed beside a window. foul weather sputters in the alleyway
and a hybrid entity of wind and rain murmurs at the windowsill. the recording refers me back to a particular place and its lighting, its smells, my actions and the environment there, and a time. the room has such conditions of its own that influence me.
it is much like i am in two places at once; not quite a simultaneity, but a feeling that time overlaps in me.

i have a fuzzy understanding of what it means to make oneself a field.

                      o

cables sag and stretch across a large area of nowhere,
facilitating a uniform surge between two rooms. slivers are thrown off like tiny spinning stars that fall slowly into the grass.
                          the siphon glimmers then is gone.

later, in another heart of the landscape, i duck and pass beneath a black cable hanging across a sunken footpath, not missing a faint emanation
           as if from some interstitial material coursing.

                    o

inside the ruin i am stirred by the ghost of human actions.
damaged wood and metal variously ajar and fallen, vast areas of mold across flecked surfaces lit by stray beams, scattered broken glass and opaque pools,
mulched paper piled with feathers and birdshit, dangling wires and conduits,
                    holes, mounds, drips, webs.

here and there the remains of personal objects resonate and remind me of the personalities that once persevered through daily life in this mill. i move about warily, brushing past tiny plants sprung from holes in the walls, dodging soft spots on the floor,
          breathing quietly as i step into the cave of a shadow.

o

i could have sat for hours beside the web-filled bore just waiting for some flutter or noise. what would a tiny ear far into that length of log make of these frosted grasses under influence of my parting footfalls

                              and the steeply-angled wind?

o

the specimens of the field resist captivity. i return with my tranquilizations and find that they ecstatically 'come to' during playback. they release in spasms similar to the ones under which they were initially coaxed from hiding. then, it is almost as if a pile of debris—rusted flecks, effluvia, twigs and splinters—has accumulated on the floor beneath the speakers.
the insides of the cones show marks where they have been singed,

                soaked,
                      beaten and scraped by wings.

the siphon rasps as the days spill themselves onto the hard edges of the room.

o

many days after my setting out, just as the breadth of my loneliness was becoming unwieldy, i heard a solitary and playful laughter emanate from an opening in the trees. it is hard at moments like these not to give in to thoughts of the supernatural offering itself, intimately, to you and you alone. this woman's voice coming through the trees was much like an isolate and palely glowing door, inwardly ajar like an invitation onto some adjacent world. having allowed myself these glimmers of fantasy, i now wished only that it was someone much like myself, purposefully afoot in the landscape in pursuit of some curiosity, evidence of some belief, and that we might travel for a short while together.

when at last i stepped into the clearing there was nobody to be seen. momentarily some other sound began surmounting the periphery. it was as if everything that had ever passed through my ears was coming to some ecstatic culmination in which i no longer played a part.

> home again
> i am sound.

Mark Wallace

Looking Beyond the Fields of Poetry

An earlier version of this piece was presented at the conference on Societies of American Poetry: Dissenting Practices, held at Georgetown University February 20-22, 2003.

    Why do I think we should question what it means to conceive of poetry as a field? What makes me leap so quickly to skepticism? All descriptive terms create a lens through which the object under consideration—whether it's an object or not—becomes viewed. Such descriptive terms make new ways of seeing possible, but they equally limit, probably even prevent, other ways of seeing. When we think of poetry as a field, what do we see? Just as importantly, what do we not see? What is the impact of this concept of "the field" on the social presence—and the other possible presences—of poetry?

    Perhaps a quick look at some prominent notions in the last century of poetry as a field would help. For T.S. Eliot in "Tradition and the Individual Talent," the field of poetry becomes a discrete set of poems and poets that have met the highest standards, standards which involve for Eliot an overcoming of personal and cultural limitations in order to have one's writing merge with what Matthew Arnold had called, not too many years earlier, "the best that has been thought and said." In this view, which we call these days the concept of "the canon," very few poems and poets actually become part of the field of poetry—most are destined never to belong. The field of the canon, a field of monuments in which now and then another monument goes up, becomes recognizable by the way its monuments rise above the refuse of language—and bodies—that must be washed clear of its meticulously kept grounds. The field of poetry becomes a garden of the best.

In a time when at least some writers are aware that poetry involves multiple standards, histories, and cultures, anthropology and more recently cultural studies have offered expanded models of the field of poetry. In these models, poetry becomes broadly speaking an object of culture, both a reflection of lived experience and a comment on it. The poet, in these models, might be described as a culture worker, making a series of objects which reveal their intimate involvement with many types of cultural meaning. There are obvious dangers in such a perspective, especially in terms of the historical split between anthropologist and the culture under study; it was for this reason that in graduate school, I once referred to British critic Anthony Easthope's 1983 book *Poetry as Discourse* as "Poetry as Primitive Culture." The poet becomes too easily seen as a strange creature, fascinating in her desire not to conform to institutional standards, but ultimately explainable and in need of explaining both to us and perhaps, also, to herself. By now of course the cultural studies model has made things more subtle, granting the culture worker a legitimate intellectual and social status; the poet as culture worker becomes a complex, contradictory, but often heroic struggler against cultural and economic oppression. The best poets become those who understand most clearly their relationship to class, race, gender constructs and the mechanics of domination, as well as related crucial issues like ecology and war.

As far as I know, Pierre Bourdieu has not written more than briefly on the culture work of poets. But his concept of cultural capital can be extrapolated to offer another sense of poetry as a field. For Bordieu, all of us who work in ideas, poets or otherwise, are involved in a struggle for cultural capital; that is, we all want our fields taken more seriously by others, and we all want more resources available to our fields. As poets, we both struggle within our field for this limited cultural capital—poets compete for readers, book opportunities, grants, academic positions—but also, as members of a field, we struggle with members of other fields. And we struggle with the world at large as well—as poets, we want our voices heard, not just about poetry, because we believe what we say should have more impact.

What's especially intriguing about all this is that, for Bordieu, the struggle for cultural capital can be more or less measured. Poets, and poems, have changed particular things in particular circumstances, and have not changed things in other circumstances, and this impact, although at times amorphous, can for its most significant part be determined. The field of poetry is defined by the history of the social effect of poetry on the world. The power of poets can be compared to the power of historians, accountants, economists, factory owners. This analysis, for Bordieu, probably puts to rest all vague propaganda about "the power of the creative act"— we can determine what that power is, literally.

But when I think about Bourdieu's sense of measure, I am reminded always of Jack Spicer: "No one listens to poetry." We know, obviously, that what Spicer says isn't true. But we also know, even if we don't want to, that it's true *enough*. The power of poetry to impact, even change the world is clear, but equally clear is its limited ability to do so. If we believe that the field of poetry is defined by its measurable social impact, at least some people will decide—rightly—that poetry may not be the best way to have that impact, or that poetry is only one of an array of activities (and how important a one, exactly?) necessary to achieve it. The particular crisis that this issue represents for poetry occurs repeatedly; the critique that poetry and poets need to become more political, more activist, to do more, is a critique of poetry that in my lifetime (much longer than that, in fact) has never for a single moment stopped, even though too many poets act like they're the first to notice it or bring it up. My point is that such critique never stops because it's true; when it comes to measurable social impact, poetry doesn't do enough. Poets are too small a social group—not to mention too conflicted or recalcitrant—and poems are not read enough, quite simply. Yes, poetry should have more impact.

However, Robert Duncan's "Opening of the Field," both the book and the concept, suggests another notion of field, one which may provide some alternatives to the limitations, perhaps frustrations, of the notions I've been discussing. The field of poetry becomes, first, the physical space of the page on which language appears, but also, by extension, the material fact of the world, and all the ways language reflects, responds to, and creates those material facts. Poetry becomes not simply a field of discrete objects, or of culture workers and what they create, or the measurable social power of those workers and creations. Instead, it becomes an exploration of how language permeates the world—but also an exploration of the other ways that language *could* permeate the world. Poetry offers not simply a field of study, not simply a social or institutional discipline that one can enter with the goal of improving the cultural capital of one's ideas and their virtues. Poetry becomes not solely a field defined by its disciplinary role relative to other fields, but also the very suggestion that language can, must, and will be rewritten—that even the concept of the field is, at best, for poetry and other fields as well, our own temporary understanding, one full of great possibilities but also shocking limits.

Perhaps that sounds terribly amorphous, too much like a generalization about creative acts, or the cliche that "poetry can save your life." But I think it isn't. If poetry is, certainly, a field in all the ways I have discussed—a contested but definite discipline of study, a contested field of power—then it is also one of the few human activities in which the very idea of fields cannot simply be critiqued but also moved beyond, however temporarily or by example only. Yes, poets can critique, dissent, struggle, and they should, but so can workers in any other field, and in that sense, poetry is no more than one of many important fields, and the poet who looks only to poetry for his sources of dissent is at best intensely limited by his concept of the field.

What poetry can do, however, that no other field can do so well, is to offer new modes of language, different ways of writing one's engagement with the world, not a field of study only but a way of living and writing that can never be contained by the dynamics of fields and their struggles. Poetry cannot always change the world. But it can, sometimes, show us what a changed world might look like. It can show us what kinds of writing and thinking, and the people who write and think them, are forgotten when we believe poetry is a field solely defined by a struggle for power. Every time we decide that our parameters for knowing poetry are what it is, or that the uses we make of it are the only value it has, we have limited poetry to the idea of a field that poetry itself ultimately flows past. Poetry can critique and dissent, but as part of that dissent and beyond it, it can also reach out, reach through, spin, sing, thunder, torque, fragment, cry, connect, strip, hold, destroy, carry. Poetry can offer us the full complexity of the possibilities through which we live in language, and the idea of the field is, at best, only one of such possibilities. Speaking of poetry as a field defines the limits of what it can do in a world of fields; it shows us the terror that poetry certainly must confront. Speaking of what poetry can otherwise do shows us all the ways in which the world is not a series of fields, but something also stranger, more beautiful, more capable of changing, and more uncontainable by the current limits of what passes for the social world and our understanding of it.

Dale Smith

IN TIME: JOANNE KYGER
AND THE NARRATIVE OF EVERY DAY

An hour north of San Francisco and situated on a mesa between the Bolinas lagoon and the Pacific Ocean, the township of Bolinas was an ideal hippie arcadia dominated by great dope, wonderful company, creative living and scenic excursions. At one time Jim Carroll, Robert Creeley, *Paris Review* editor Tom Clark, *New American Poetry* editor Donald Allen, poets David Meltzer and Duncan McNaughton, artist Arthur Okamura and many other writers, musicians and artists lived together in this flower power paradise. The Bolinas-based *Coyote's Journal*, edited by Jim Koller and Bill Brown, published important work by Anselm Hollo, Edward Dorn, Allen Ginsberg, Gary Snyder and others. It also published *High Grade*, doodles and poems by Philip Whalen, another West Coast poet whose work pushed narrative structure in new directions. Bill Berkson's Big Sky press, Donald Allen's Four Seasons Foundation and Michael Wolfe's *Tombouctou* were all publishing poetry well into the 1980s. While the vibrant and exciting scene of the 1960s and '70 has diminished in Bolinas, it remains a gorgeous outpost for those artists and writers who have made homes on land that once belonged to Miwok Indians, and other Northern Coast tribes.

Joanne Kyger's work is central to the history of the Bolinas writing community, (not to mention the larger national and international poetry communities), and in many ways it is indicative of the kinds of attention to narrative practiced by New Americans during the 1960s and '70s. A sense of place is key to her work. Of prime importance to generations of young writers, her house continues to be a kind of hearth for visiting poets. She has made her home in Bolinas since the late 1960s. Prior to that, she lived and traveled in Japan and India with Gary Snyder, with whom she developed a lifelong practice of Zen that continues to influence her work. Part of the San Francisco Renaissance of poets in the '50s, she frequented North Beach bars with Jack Spicer, Robert Duncan, George Stanley and others in an apprenticeship of extraordinary depth and energy.

Her work is prominent in the 1971 City Lights publication of *On The Mesa: An Anthology of Bolinas Writing*. (A blurb by Daniel Moore for the book is indicative of the idealistic and hopeful spirit focused on Bolinas at this time: "&so these poets have taken to the Bolinas Mesa, high ground, while the world goes awash around them, practising a little 'Black Mountainery,' a little 'New York Schoolery,' and a little Tom Foolery. All a part of America's vital poetic machinery, high on the Mesa.") One of her poems is dedicated to Ebbe Borregaard, another New American who appears with Kyger in this anthology. Tom Clark in turn dedicates one of his poems to her, showing not only the closeness of the community in Bolinas, but acknowledging the primary force Kyger's presence is to them as writers. One of Creeley's contributions to the anthology, "'Bolinas and Me,'" refers to her briefly when he writes, "I remember Joanne. I / want to. She's / lovely, one says. / So she is." (29) Donald Allen published his Four Seasons Foundation from Bolinas at this time too, solidly identifying the little Marin County village with the New American poetry he initiated into print in 1960. The confluence of Beats, Black Mountaineers, San Francisco Renaissancers and New York school poets made Bolinas a unique backwater where geographic isolation provided creative energy, experimentation, discussion, communal dialogue and play. No doubt it generated infighting, bickering, and various jealousies and enraged, drunken, drug-fuelled acts of depraved emotional intensities. The scene itself would collapse as one-by-one many of the poets moved away, abandoned the writing of poems or retreated into hermetic isolation. But for a time, Bolinas provided a rich ground where artists could listen and learn from each other. Such work in common relations led to diverse responses. A new kind of narrative was one primary result.

"I discovered that Thoreau had defined a 'day book' as a literal record of the day's activities and thoughts," wrote Creeley in his introduction to *Mabel: A Story*, "without attempt to understand or digest or to reflect upon them. That was perfectly my own intent." (*Collected Prose*, 266) It is notable here that Creeley links himself to a greater American narrative tradition. Prior to the New Americans, there were many examples of daybook narratives, and Thoreau's remains an idiosyncratic, rich and provocative example of one man's attention to the rhythm and progression of days. Walt Whitman's *Specimen Days* is another example of prose fragments, portraits and penetrations into memory, his Civil War experience and old age. But by the 1950s and '60s, the form and uses of a daybook were beginning to move more directly into the novels and creative prose experiments of Jack Kerouac, William Burroughs and others. Creeley would makes prose and verse poems most notably in *A Day*

Book (Scribner, 1972) and *Pieces* (Scribner 1969). On the East Coast James Schuyler's marvelous attentions were recorded in journals, and the visual clarity and adoration of mundane days dominated many of his most memorable poems. William Corbett's *Columbia Square Journal* (Angel Hair, 1976) records in brief verse notes one year between Columbus Day 1974 and '75. Paul Blackburn's *Journals* (Black Sparrow, 1975) and John Ashbery's *The Vermont Notebook* (Black Sparrow, 1975) also reflect the influence of daybook narrative structures on poets related to the New Americans. In California, Philip Whalen and Joanne Kyger took the form farthest; incorporating it into a lifelong pursuit of poetry that demanded spiritual perfection and provisory relations to environment and experiences in it.

Kyger is a frank and inspiring conversationalist. Through years of deep practice of poetry and Zazen, as well as the manners and courtesies of village life in Bolinas, she has managed to compress in pragmatic fashion questions or statements that clear the air in an instant.

"I don't care what someone knows or feels," she said to me once in conversation about poetry, "I want to know what's happening."

I repeat this because it impressed me deeply, and it corresponds with Creeley's statement above. It also reveals much that is true of the new narrative forms that came out of the 1960s and '70s in and around Bolinas. Particularly, the statement draws attention to Kyger's own careful, perceptive nature and her uses of poetry. Rather than the well-crafted, overly-wrought and fretted-over, metaphor-driven and exhausted poems often published in places like the New Yorker, Kyger exemplifies a faith in the life-long process of self preparation, trust in the poem and its instantaneous recognition in the projective field à la Charles Olson. Unlike Olson, however, she focuses on events and happenings, moving herself out of the way except as a kind of recording instrument. Philip Whalen, from whom she learned much, demands a similar ethos. His finished poems, however, are more like seamless, well-crafted collages from notebooks. They are full of humor and detached observations of divers physical and creative environments. Kyger's work by contrast is personally intimate, faithful to specific moments in time and attendant to the diverse spirits or moods of landscape. The real difference, perhaps, is the frame of attention, and the spirits guiding it. Whalen's curmudgeonly genius contrasts starkly with Kyger's bright and socially centered persona.

Her attention to place makes her an intimate observer of everyday life in her beloved Bolinas. Her engagement with organic life processes is mirrored by the visual construction of her poems on the page, where lines often are set out into the space of the page rather than stacked along the left-hand margin. In this sense visually she is close to Pound and Williams, using the page as a kind of painting or glyph for the ease and pleasure of the eye.

"I saw the page as some kind of tapestry and voice glyph," she said in a 1997 interview, echoing concerns for the poem that have been with her from her first book, *The Tapestry and the Web*. "When you move your line to the right, the lesser the impact of the line, the voice. The whole movement and rhythm on the page give us instruction as to voice and phrasing and import of what's going on."

In this interview I conducted with her in Bolinas, she addressed her concerns for writing or creative environments, how anything can become part of a person's poetic practice.

"Your dreams are important," she said, "your humorous life is important, your cooking life is important, your friendships, the dialogues you assume, the news that comes from within, the news that comes from out there. There's such a wide variety of 'things' that go on. It's important not to get stuck on any one of these as being the 'I' that writes. Being able to report, as it were, from all these areas of life and see that they're equally 'valid' and 'important.' Nothing is more or less important than anything else. An egalitarian sense of what it's like to be a human. What being alive is like."

This kind of attention to divers aspects of domestic, private and public life is noted casually by her in notebooks. It's a use of attention that is different from traditional narrative structures that are based on arbitrary structures of time to create an illusion of continuity. Her observations take seriously the content of every day, making poems from spiral-bound notebooks in which she notes daily happenings, events and impressions.

"In this daily writing," she said, "you don't have to think of it as 'poetry,' you don't have to think at all about what 'kind' of writing you're doing. You're writing some kind of un-self-conscious open utterance, being as clear as you can, or as muddled as you want. You're not writing for anybody. It's spontaneous."

Through this process, the otherness of language becomes apparent.

Words and especially those words arranged in the open field of the poem, for Kyger, reveal perceptions that disrupt, challenge and surprise her own thoughts. Because in journal writing, unlike often in poetry, there is a detachment from language in an effort to record eventuality, language finds a unique freedom from personal constraint and purpose. A shift of intent to experience and away from the inner chambers of self gives language a freedom and openness through which novelty can enter.

"Words have their own independent existence," she said. "They say what they want to. Like Spicer saying you are just the medium, the funnel for the words to go through. They have their own lineage, returning through you. The magic syllables, seed syllables."

o

The poems presented recently in *As Ever: Selected Poems* (Penguin 2002), span more than 40 years, and often in the work Bolinas is focused through Kyger's keen eye. The daybook quality of the work creates a narrative from the fabric of every day life. Early poems from her first book, *The Tapestry and the Web*, project the story from Homer of Odysseus' homecoming onto her own domestic and personal relations. She attempts her own weaving of myth into personal experience to register a condition in poetry that will return years later more naked and less forced. *Tapestry*, though, is an extraordinary presentation of a poet's early work. Simply, she seeks an alignment of heaven and earth, the presence of myth in the present. She registers myth as an organizing formal energy of every day life. Her poems too are a complex occasion of forces, with humor and lightness of touch easing more serious relations and insights.

"Refresh my thought of Penelope again," she writes, "Just HOW / solitary was her wait? / I notice Someone got to her that / barrel chested he-goat prancing / around w/ his reed pipes / is no fantasy of small talk." (*As Ever*, 10)

Kyger always shows you what's happening where she is, proceeding in language from divers environments. Physical landscapes, travel notes, flora and fauna flourish in her provocative writing. Details of life in Japan, Mexico and Bolinas emerge through these bright poems. The body of her work in a way reads like an ongoing daybook, a form she has transformed and extended through the compression and careful selection of her words. Kyger shares affinities with Lady Murasaki's *The Pillow Book*, to root the formal inspiration for her writing in the deeper past. The new uses of narrative practiced by the New American generation of the 1950s and '60s extended methods of writing based on chance accumulations, thoughts and captured experiences taken down casually in notebooks. While Creeley's *A Day Book*, Paul Blackburn's *Journals* and William Corbett's *Columbia Square Journal* exemplify this trend in specific books, Kyger, who often dates her poems, has consistently worked within the daybook format for more than 40 years. Her prolonged engagement with narrative is unique. By attending time closely and slowly, she confronts and disrupts her "self" through a process of careful observation, selection and relations of daily phenomena over periods of several years. Her proposed marriage of heaven and earth in *The Tapestry and the Web* continues in later poems, but without the need for mythological or literary grounding. There is even an anti-literary quality to her work. She takes as subject what the day presents, in all its mundane, domestic and often extraordinary presence. In "Morning Mess" she writes:

> Just waiting to go out there and boogie it up
> In case anyone comes by
>
> *Everybody practices magic*
>   whether they know it or not
> Oh I'm worn out
>   just watching the cats
> lick their fur
>   I'm worn out
>   fading fast
>   my *hair* is arranged
>   the boon of illimitable life is obtained.

(*As Ever*, 169)

Fundamentally, she is a religious poet. Besides a serious study and practice of Zazen, her poems are disruptive of her own satisfaction or comfort with herself, thus opening her to a provisory existence. This character trait prevents her work from reaching the smug heights often displayed in the writing of the Official Verse Culture supported by mainstream journals, university departments and granting foundations. But through poetry she can penetrate beyond personal complexities, moods and ideas, tending immediate environments instead, and emotionally reckoning in an instant the rich fabric of life's threads.

> These several selves that move one self around, thousands jiggling. It is so inappropriate to be unfound, whine

> around, hesitate, lock the window again, this body is
> dissipated. To accomplish, to learn, with thanks, to one's
> past history is brought up close. And for a while, with
> late spring's wild radish flower blooming past my window,
> the further shore is close, is here. I do not want to say
> he is dead yet because he has not yet come back, but my
> sadness for the missing comes recognised, is acceptable.
> Gone with the last look he questioned me with. Have you
> done this to me?
>
> >Indeed are they my forces or the forces
> I am within. That no children come from me to love. And I
> am this space in time, this focus, of articulation, that hears
> the bee buzz round and round. (*As Ever,* 143)

The sudden shifts of tone in her poems show a dramatic and clear perceptive range. Intense self-scrutiny and humorous self-commentary are often intertwined. Cultural and religious references are woven into a physical landscape. Turkey buzzards are totem familiars that appear in her poems as they do in the skies above her mesa, suddenly surprising, full of mystery and charm. Northern California predominately emerges as a great force, its vivid landscape and Pacific Ocean, the mesa, grasses and mountains all reveal a phenomenalogical pressure of candid detail and personal measure. The distinctions between self, body and landscape, God and domestic gods of place blend into the vibrant fabric of every day.

The titles of her books also give clues to her art: *Joanne* (Angel Hair, 1970), *Places to Go* (Black Sparrow, 1970), *Trip Out and Fall Back* (Arif Press, 1974), *The Wonderful Focus of You* (Z Press, 1980), *Up*

My Coast (Floating Island Publications, 1981) and *Some Life* (The Post Apollo Press, 2000) are just a few. These works contribute to the daybook-like narrative; an extended tale of days lived, not remembered or projected upon. She is a pioneer in American letters of a new narrative approach that is grounded in personal experience. Like other Beat comrades she is politically and socially fierce, but underneath, forming the basis of her breath, is a religious push to be in the world naked or close to naked every day, participating to the fullness of one's self.

"Watching TV", like many of her poems, exhibits on a first reading a deceptive ease. The form is open, conversational, visually intriguing, composed as if by "field"—to use the language of Olson's "Projective Verse", an essay that Kyger first encountered in 1957. "Watching TV" also evinces her accuracy of image and language.

> Ahoy! electronic nightmare . . .
> You don't see many Skunks watching TV
> that is,   if you are watching the tube
> you never get to see Skunk outside strolling
> in the full moon towards the compost. Good Evening.
> He lifts his tail. I'm just strolling, so all is well
> with the smell. (*As Ever*, 272)

The skunk leads us into the poem, to the poet's living room. Televised images are vomited as from a worm's mouth against the striking, potentially stinking, image of that skunk. The little beast shakes up Kyger's routine, calling attention to the habit of television, manifesting a surprising form in the dark outdoors. More than just a skunk, the creature is an instance of the cosmic pattern as perceived, with noted humor, by the poet. It realigns her sense of mission within the mundane domestic blast of TV.

A trusty recorder of daily life, Kyger approaches the quotidian and the sublime via subtle observations. She can present a landscape, say, with sudden strokes, letting image settle next to image provocatively. In "View North," a poem to the memory of poet Larry Eigner, she writes: "Back dropped / blue-grey clouds / warm lull / a spot of sun / in this clearing / of moment transferred— / a perfectly peaceful point / of view." Here the compression of her lines and the sonic charge of her vowels complicate and deepen the poem with a resonance beyond mere scenic description. Language also is a process of self-inquiry, the poetic field a space for the disruptions and intrusions essential to discovering the unknown content within herself and the physical or creative environments she inhabits by force. The language she brings to those every day moments reveals and relates the world in her scrutiny of diverse forms.

In a sense, the skunk in "Watching TV" was inside Kyger all along, released by the television to rummage around in her yard. And in possession of the image, a skunk enters a poem, liberated from the unknown content inside herself. The visitation leads to a "topographical enlightenment," opening the poet's eyes to the simple charms of the night sky, "the promenade of crisp hedges." "'The world / around us is workable' when the mind / is unfettered and away from the tube, the screen; / the eyeball engaged in a back lighted room—mind tomb." In Kyger's, the mind, trapped at first within the gridlock of daily routine and social demands, is interrupted; attention is redirected, through the breath of the poem, to the natural world.

Notably left out of recent anthologies, including *The Norton Anthology of Postmodern American Poetry* and *Moving Borders: an anthology of innovative writing by women*, Kyger's work has challenged consistent, linear narrative effect by working with time rather than against time. That is, she doesn't project her conception of the world through it, she uses time as a lens through which, slowly, experience of the world is sharpened. She is, as Ron Silliman notes, "one of our hidden treasures—the poet who really links the Beats, the Spicer Circle, the Bolinas poets, the NY School and the language poets, and the only poet who can be said to do all of the above." Beyond such lineages and linkages, she is a religious poet with a demanding intelligence. Language is the medium between her and the world, the poetic field her space for registering the unknown content of both. Through a consistent and prolonged practice she has discovered narrative possibilities that open the world through language. Her attention, whether turned to her domestic Bolinas, Zazen, California coastal Indians or the Theosophist Madame Blavatsky, retrieves a writing that uses time as an ally and guide. Her words show an opening into many worlds. Narrative for her is Gnosis, knowledge of what's happening in time.

Kristen Hanlon

ELIZABETH WILLIS, *Turneresque*
Burning Deck, 2003

On the back cover of Elizabeth Willis's latest book, in lieu of blurbs or bio, is an exhortation from Rimbaud: "THE WORLD MARCHES ON! WHY SHOULDN'T IT TURN AROUND?" Some of the turns these poems negotiate: from thinking to singing, from idea to act, from realism to impressionism, from painter J.M.W. Turner to media mogul Ted Turner. Whether her vehicle is verse or the postcard-size prose poem, *Turneresque* resonates with a kind of restless music; these are poems to drive to.

    In the verse sections of the collection, description takes a backseat to abstraction. Willis floods poems like "Sonnet" with inventive metaphors and similes: "Grammar is coral/a gabled light/against the blue/a dark museum/durable thing"; "Your dream above your head/like comic weather". In "Elegy", a Steinian definition: "(T)he mind's a hinge/a roughly chestnut arsenal/a little box of nothing/an incidental rose." When Willis uses the first-person, she chooses an "I" that is dislocated, amorphous: "The present was a relic/of a past/I was older than//Taking its language, I became an abridgement/of whatever I contained" ("Autographeme"). In "Ingrid Washinawatok", this changeable "I" naturally extends itself to a reincarnation scenario: "I'm sure I'll come back/as a spider someone like me/will crush and send to sea/or the ant endlessly/walking my ceiling."

At the heart of the book is a section of prose poems that pay homage to over a dozen B-movies of the 1940s and 1950s. Each poem is titled for the movie it summarizes, and appropriates the "tough guy" language and irony of the film noir. However, these are summaries with a twist, showing there's a poet at work, not a film critic: "Her brother's heart is an inward tree, but he's got blood on his hands. Love gropes more than blossoms." ("On Dangerous Ground"). "She gets loved by accident, the one without frosting. Her sex is deep and refracted. She can hold her own at sea." ("A Stolen Life"). By keeping in the present tense and using clipped, humorous, noir-ish phrasings, Willis makes each poem unfold as if we're watching the movie ourselves.

The final section of the book is comprised of an 11-section prose poem, "Drive". Each part of the poem is like a landscape quickly glimpsed from the window of a moving car. Accordingly, the poem shifts location even as key words (fire, dirt, leaf, heart) are repeated. It's a very American poem in the sense that it is simultaneously preoccupied with moving/exile and with finding or returning to an idealized "home": "What you rise out of may not be dirt, but what you breathe must be air. On an indigo chart, we rise without a future, left to wish outside the forward rush of things. Who would not leave the mess for the illumination, the culture for the poem?" Who, indeed? The disillusioned citizen, the itinerant academic? Perhaps both. The accomplished poems of *Turneresque* succeed by, as Willis puts it in "Elegy", "Threading a life/of levered paradox."

Brian Teare

JOSELY VIANNA BAPTISTA, *On the Shining Screen of the Eyelids*. Translated by Chris Daniels.
Manifest Press, 2003.

While reading Josely Vianna Baptista's book, *On the Shining Screen of the Eyelids,* I was called back to the essay "Indirect Language and the Voices of Silence," by Maurice Merleau-Ponty. Perhaps because Baptista's poetry's textural hybridity explores equally both visual and aural resources of language via a typographical experiment that's also full of rhyme and alliteration. Or perhaps because of the appealingly eccentric way in which the imagery and eclectic diction of the poems' fabric enact a complex weave of what is eye and what is mind ("Eye and Mind" being another of Merleau-Ponty's essays). Or perhaps, and also more to the point, because Baptista's project is finally one in which, as Merleau-Ponty writes,

> Language is oblique and autonomous, and if it sometimes signifies a thought or a thing directly, that is only the secondary power derived from its inner life. Like the weaver, the writer works on the wrong side of the material. He has to do only with language, and it is thus that he suddenly finds himself surrounded by meaning. (82)

It's difficult to describe to why Baptista's poems call forth the metaphor of weaving, this working "on the wrong side of the material," without reproducing their layout. But before I quote their typography directly, let me try.

Baptista's poetry—since it appears to be composed on the sentence level, without relying on the traditional poetic line as a measure—could be described as prose-poetry were it not for the typography it employs. Most of the poems in *On the Shining Screen of the Eyelids* use the ample pages' white space not so much as fields, but rather as weaver's looms of white thread upon which figures, or perhaps more accurately, figurations, arise at the place where eye and mind, warp and weft, touch, language the shuttle that binds them. Using only typographer's colors, the base matter of words—letters—is separated by white space, the effect of which is that words themselves appear both elongated and aerated, both given more space and inhabited by space until the quality that distinguishes Baptista's poetry—its simultaneous density and airiness—appears. It is no accident that her first volume of poetry is titled *Air*.

And what artifice determines the appearance of the words themselves affects also the sentence and its syntax: individual marks of punctuation operate inside their own whiteness, and syntax often stretches over the entire span of a poem's printed lines, which themselves are double-spaced, and thus framed on all sides by white space. In keeping with calling to the readers' attention the absolute artifice of each material—white space, letter, punctuation, word, phrase—of which a poem is made, each poem also brings to the attention its frame due to the large format of the book, and also because of the variable size of the poems: some fill the page quite densely, while others, very small, call attention to their presentation as though they were objets d'art, back-lit, on display.

In some cases, this kind of visual airiness produces the peculiar density felt when reading Baptista's work: it's the density of time, what Baptista calls "that net of ellipses," being slowed down (52). Often, because individual words must be broken between printed lines to accommodate white space, the reader must wait to finish a word's meaning. And strangely, though the poems don't make use of the traditional connotations of lineated verse, the effect of white space stretching syntax over many printed lines is often that of lineation: meaning is again delayed, and, in grammatically dependent phrases, momentarily lost or distorted. It is almost as if, in reading these poems, syntax itself were "the body that returns to being time," as Baptista writes later in the book (75).

Thus the beauty of Baptista's typography is that, where meaning is concerned, white space functions both visually and aurally: it is both absence and silence, and the page acts as "the background of silence which does not cease to surround [the word] and without which it would say nothing" (Merleau-Ponty 83).

And that, if writing is a mediation between silence and speech, is where Baptista's work calls to mind Merleau-Ponty's injunction that "we must uncover the threads of silence with which speech is intertwined" (84).

On a thematic and imagistic level, Baptista's work accomplishes this by being dedicated to the world and its materiality, and drawing a large share of her imagery from landscape, whether pastoral, geological or marine. However, these landscapes are almost always parsed into constituent parts—the "frost, jade, jasper" of "chill pre-dawn, landscape"—and fraught with juxtapositions with the artificial or immaterial, such as when "frost, jade, jasper" are, later on in the poem, arranged "on the skin of a landscape" (27).

Thus Baptista, "wishing," as she writes of herself, "a fight, a chimera, the odd rigor, the rare rhyme," self-consciously filters the world—what is seen—through her language—what is thought and written—rendering a sense of being that is itself marvelously chimerical, a radical linguistic mix of the organic and the artificial (19).

This means that, in a poem like "chill pre-dawn, landscape" for example, there is no such thing as landscape per se; rather, there is "landscape seen through landscape," and that when the poet assembles her palimpsest of the literal and the figurative, it is full of doublings, of couplings, and of permutations of repetition that transform "air upon air into ars":

> chill pre-dawn, landscapes
> een through landscape, frost
> , jasper shard seems jade, f
> rost's gauze hazes landscap
> e, jasper shade seems jad
> e, proliferant jasper on f
> rosty landscape in a vip
> er's husk, in the waltz o
> f a wasp, in a billboa
> rd's tatter, in a poem'
> s aura, in mineral smoke

> from a speaker's mout
> h, air upon air into ar
> s condensing an image
> , frost, jade, jasper on
> the skin of a landscape
> waiting's harshness al
> ters in mirage : ants tr
> ace tracks in flour
> (27)

"chill pre-dawn, landscape," which is from Air, seems to me exemplary of Baptista's ability to usher imagery from the material world into a linguistic space that hovers, deliciously, between forms of the referential and the mediated. This mode of writing, with its rhymes and repetitive phrasing, draws an almost hallucinatory scrim— a state of hyper-referentiality—over ordinary nouns so that, in an accretive fashion, "frost's gauze hazes landscape" until the phrase "jasper shard seems jade" becomes "jasper shade seems jade." When she later claims that "frost, jade, jasper on the skin of a landscape waiting's harshness alters in mirage," she demonstrates the deft blend of descriptive and discursive writing that allows her to move so quickly between eye and mind, the writing taking place as it does in an eternal present tense where, as she writes elsewhere, "parasol's watergreen darkens and rain threads down . . . as if time vanished in that ash" (75).

Another distinguishing characteristic of these poems, and another sign of their absolute dedication to materiality, is their eclectic, encyclopedic diction, admirably rendered by Daniels' translations. Drawing from the Latinate language of biological sciences—ocelli, vibrissae, primulae, silex, murices, corundum—and from the various language roots of archaic cultures—menhir, dolmen, haruspicial—the poems also employ a diction dedicated to the whorls, colors, and curlicues of artifice and language, what Daniels in his introduction calls Baptista's baroque leanings—pensile, logogriphs, opaline, volutes, hieroglyphs. However, this lavish materiality is countered by an equal number of abstractions, often in reference to absence—nullities, nil, void, vortex, abyss, nichts— wherein we see Baptista, "between preterit and horizon," trying to tease out the relationship of absence to presence (51).

This juxtaposition works beautifully throughout the book, demonstrating the tension that exists in language between the realms of eye and mind—"nothing's nothing, not even a mist of nothing" (71)—or in language used to describe lover and beloved plagued by circumstance and time: "in the fleeting brilliance returned by your face viewed through sheets of glass that far bear the gaze, bear hows, bear whens, hours throwing bolts in the body that returns to being time . . . as if void so vanished in that ash, as if it vanished, it were, as if it" (76). Occasionally, the "baroque" quality of the diction errs on the side of purple prose, such as when this passage seems to wander onto the set of a scene worthy of Revelations: "silica silence binds the sky into a book reflecting shafts of purple moon, black sun, on absinthe waters where angels of the abyss recite the dead names of seven thousand men, and on the deserted ocean words swim among waves" (79). However, this kind of overwriting doesn't occur often, and what it allows Baptista when it works is a simultaneity of subjective high Romance and objective critical detachment, the paradoxical foundation upon which her project is built.

Heightening the dialogue between eye and mind that so pervades and problematizes the writing itself, Baptista's texts, in the book's second half, are interspersed with pencil drawings by Francisco Faria. Excerpted from Baptista's second book, *Corpography*, the poems and imagery are part of a visual-poetic collaboration between the two artists, and given that Faria's meticulous work juxtaposes marine and jungle landscapes with nudes whose backs contain text or figuration, the introduction of visual art into the book serves to enhance and counterpoint Baptista's interest in the intersections between subjectivity, writing, and landscape. Because Faria's images introduce each of the three sections of *Corpography*, the pairing is perhaps most striking at the opening of the first section, where we move from a drawing incorporating text to the first poem, which begins: "lion-hued the drawing of a verse phosphoresces in darkness" (49).

And indeed the title *Corpography* itself is emblematic, for often Baptista's writing intends to chart the meeting of lover and beloved in the gap between "peril, paradise" (35): "the golden mean of chaos in secret repeats the glare the pleasure of your skewed body, on fire, keeps from swooning out of my gaze" (53). It is here, where "from under chestnut voile my down shown blond by the sun," that "your tongue embroiders voids onto silence," and "thinking [is] suspended" (53). And it is here, where the lover's gaze meets both beloved and landscape, that the problem of the gaze, of eye and mind, is, if not completely "suspended," at least given its share of eros: "the fever of your eyes folding fanlike, rolling primulae enrolled on the marge, become storm: landscape's oilblack" (73). It is one of the pure pleasures of the book: that the forms of subjectivity—thought, gaze, language—like beaten iron in the smith's workshop, cool only when submerged, beneath the "vandal waves in us, adrift" (73).

Baptista's book is one of a number of recent excellent English translations from Mexican, Central, and South American writers—notable among them Maria Negroni's *Islandia* and *Night Journey*, Pura López-Colomé's *No Shelter*, Jaime Saenz's *Immanent Visitor*, and Cecilia Vicuña's *Instan*. Given the contentious atmosphere of U.S. poetics, with its decades-old, calcified debates about to what use writers should or should not put artifice, it can come as a kind of relief to read texts exploring the dimensions of other discussions. But it is, ultimately, not a relief at all that such texts offer, but a gift of dislocating the starting point of our own discussions: a gift Baptista calls an "idea against your disgeography" (49). And so we can't know yet just how lucky we are that Daniels has translated these texts, which are at liberty to declare, with a tone half insouciance, half diagnosis: "it's all just so past artifice : it'd be a fossil if it weren't an onset, a moth if not a missile" (31).

Works Cited
Merleau-Ponty, Maurice. *The Merleau-Ponty Aesthetics Reader*. Edited by Galen A. Johnson. Evanston: Northwestern University Press, 1993.

Craig Morgan Teicher

JOHN ISLES, *Ark*
University of Iowa Press, 2003

John Isles' greatest gift is the visionary pressure he exerts on the world by observing it. The poems in *Ark*, Isles' first book and a new addition to the University of Iowa Press Kuhl House Poets series, gives the peculiar sensation of simultaneous realism and allegorical inventiveness. The poems seem to invent the world while they report from it slant. We hear Stevens in playful but heady images like "the general trees of my understanding," but also know that these trees were first seen outside rather than in the mind.

These poems move quickly; the syntax jerks and surprises the reader as in this line from "Elegy to the Present Moment:" The stone begat by stone, stone/ with its placard, Washington, to paraphrase,/ passed here in his way to somewhere else." By the time the sentence comes into focus, it has already planted its sense inside the reader's mind, as though the consciousness of the speaker is a little ahead of grammar. Isles' sentences sometimes run together as though they can't contain themselves. Elsewhere, short, sharp statements are shimmied into the poems like jabs as in the following passage from "Small Traveling Islands:"

> I have lived through two forevers now:
> a forever of cowering until you sobered.
> A forever now of china-white foam,
> a third and final forever where green

235

water smears into the blonde coast,
the dark skyline crawling up.

The jailed ocean eddies past.
It isn't Irish water. Unless
the sea is coal and thunder,

a thousand kettles untended,
a city letting loose a long-held breath...
wake of cabbage plowed under.

We can hear Plath and Lowell in a controlled, under-the-breath utterance like "It isn't Irish water," but Isles sidesteps sense long enough to allow his readers to enjoy their dizziness.

In "Sirens," a car radio vies with the ocean to be the more alluring vehicle for prophesy. The poem begins, "They call me into frenzied frequencies/ between a drive-by and a pledge drive," a typically deft Isles gesture, sweeping the vernacular into the arms of the visionary. From the radio, "The voice of wishful thinking,/ a wet-mouthed nymph, rises in stereo," begging the question, "What would I have? Lovers pressing body/ to body? Not exactly not at all." Isles wrestles with the mythologizing tendencies of our language and our culture by letting the language pull the poem into fantasy then taking his metaphors to task on their fidelity to experience. The poem closes with the radio turned off and the speaker facing the ocean: "Witness the waves against the rocks./ They will not turn the volume down./ Who is dying? What city burns?/ Only the sea, which doesn't say, can say." The poem lifts off to take in a panoramic view of time and space that only language can offer, while simultaneously keeping its feet on the ground in front of the sea "which doesn't say" anything in reference to the figurative duties imposed upon it. Throughout *Ark*, Isles holds language to this standard, enjoying its capacity to invent without forgetting its responsibilities to the world at hand.

The result of Isles' contemplation of an invented world's effect on the real one is a kind of earnest irony, a satire of language which nonetheless is made to be useful. Isles' playful earnestness is refreshing in the current poetic climate in which so much poetry disdainfully turns away from the world in favor of the imagination. In "The Evangelist of Fish," while flying in a plane and reading a "book about John Smith/ and his dream of America," the speaker asks, "If I told you that down there/ a musket is being fired at a redskin,/ that he takes off with a wave of plovers,/ would that keep the plane from going down?" Isles often questions the consoling falsehood of cause-and-effect relationships by employing this sort of hyperbole. Using a similar method in "The Old Hunting Grounds," Isles explores the roots of American mythmaking in nostalgia. The speaker describes a canoe, the touchstone for a reconciliation with "the dream of Europe's America," as "mostly/ nothing on this green wound, its ribs bared/ like a hostage, decaying into the pond." From here, the poem makes its way toward the things we associate with canoes: "it takes the shape of an unshapely mass/ mired in what was once -the way/ Hiawatha never was." Here Isles holds us accountable for the injustices caused by our language. The poem closes by putting our idealized visions of America in perspective, figuring the canoe as "queen,/ more or less, of the August rain."

"Our Daughter," a portrait of parents checking in on their sleeping child, is a prime example of Isles' ability to tell the truth by making it strange. The poem delineates the human and animal expressions of love. The family is figured as "macaques on a limb...in this setting without name or address." The speaker says the daughter "must be beautiful by now./ Inconsolable sorrow, we cradle her/ like humans, very much like humans." As though watching a nature documentary about himself, the speaker perceives the difficult struggle to love with absolute clarity.

The third section of the *Ark* is a long poem called "How the Dead Kiss," made up of a series of short lyrics. The poems elegize a father figuratively or literally lost, a childhood home which has become strange to the returning adult, and the life which passes through time, casting things aside as it goes. In "The House Changing Hands," the speaker says:

> My father, the carpenter, built the house.
> He no longer fixes the windows I break.
>
> My father, the pilgrim, left nothing behind.
> My mother left *Little House on the Prairie*.
> Sometime yesterday I walked 5 miles to school.

Time is condensed by memory; the distant past may as well be "Sometime yesterday." The son sees himself become the father, saying "These father hands are my hands" ("This Is Here, It Is Now"). In the panorama of memory, "Nothing was not a symbol" ("All the Time in the World"). "How the Dead Kiss" contains some of the best moments in the collection, however, the repeating motifs (father, house, hands, ship) hold the poems together in series but do not construct a legible narrative.

Ark is among the best recent first books I've read. Isles does not let his pursuit of style subsume the poems' subject matter, a rare quality in contemporary poetry. Verbal invention abounds throughout *Ark*, propelling Isles' inquiries into the ramifications of his vision on his experience. While loss is one of Isles' principal subjects, *Ark* is also uniquely hopeful. In the concluding poem, "In the Erogenous Zone of the Body Politic," Isles says, "I pledge allegiance to the present moment." *Ark* fulfills that pledge.

CONTRIBUTORS

MARTINE BELLEN's most recent collection of poetry, *The Vulnerability of Order*, was published by Copper Canyon Press. Her previous collection, *Tales of Murasaki and Other Poems* (Sun & Moon Press) won the National Poetry Series.

ERICA BERNHEIM is a graduate of Miami University and the Iowa Writers' Workshop and is currently a PhD candidate at the University of Illinois at Chicago. Her poems have appeared in *The Canary, Can We Have Our Ball Back, Keep Going,* and are forthcoming in *Gulf Coast*.

JULIA BLOCH grew up in Northern California and Sydney, Australia. She studied political philosophy at Carleton College and earned an M.F.A. in poetry at Mills College. Her work has appeared recently in *How2, Mirage/Period(ical), Stolen Island Review, Secret Swan,* and *Small Town*, and is forthcoming in *Kaleidoscope: An International Journal of Poetry* and the "new brutalism" anthology from *Avenue B, Involuntary Vision*. Her first chapbook of sonnets, *Problem-Solving Outline*, was released by Bigfan Press in 2003; also that year, she won the Joseph Henry Jackson Literary Award. She lives in San Francisco, where she works as an editor and writes epistolary poems to Kelly Clarkson, the tow-headed winner of the original American Idol reality TV series.

LAYNIE BROWNE's most recent books are *Pollen Memory* (Tender Buttons 2003) and a novel, *Acts of Levitation* (Spuyten Puyvil, 2002). She currently resides in Oakland, California.

Born in Czernowitz, the capital of the Bukovina (now part of the Ukraine and Rumania), in 1920, PAUL CELAN was raised in a Jewish family that insisted both on the young Paul receiving the best secular education—with the mother inculcating her love of the German language and culture—and knowledge of his Jewish roots. By 1939 he started to write and that year began to study Romance literature. In 1940 Soviet troops occupied his hometown, only to be replaced by Rumanian and German Nazi troops the next year. Celan had to work in forced labor camps, where, in the fall of 1942, he learned that his father, physically broken by the slave labor he was subjected to, had been killed by the SS. Later that winter the news reached him that his mother too had been shot. These killings, especially that of his mother, were to remain the core experience of his life. Released a year later, he remained at the Sovietized University of Czernowitz until he left the Bukovina for good in April 1945. He lived in Bucharest until December 1947, when he clandestinely crossed over to Vienna, which he left in 1948 to settle in Paris, the city that was to be his home until his suicide by drowning in the Seine in April 1970. Among Celan's major writings are *Mohn und Gedächtnis (1952), Sprachgitter (1959), Die Niemandsrose (1963), Atemwende (1967), Fadensonnen (1968), and Lichtzwang (1970)*. Three posthumous volumes of late poetry have appeared, as well as a volume of collected prose and several volumes of collected correspondence.

LOREN CHASSE is a sound artist and educator living in San Francisco whose concern in both fields is with the individual experiences of the listener. As Director of Education for sound arts organization 23five Inc. and a teacher in the San Francisco public schools, Chasse has been developing curricula and teaching programs that introduce children to the means (conceptual, poetic, and technological) for actively and imaginatively listening—where sound may become a material for catalyzing literary, social, scientific and artistic practices. In Chasse's recorded work, performances and installations, he begins with a treatment of a site and its inherent sounds as an instrument, using microphones as tools for composition. By engaging an entire performance space as a 'field', Chasse demonstrates the physicality of the gestures used to induce, record and recontextualize sound, often performing within intimate proximity to each listener's ears. In addition to his solo work, Loren Chasse collaborates in the projects Coelacanth, Thuja, the Blithe Sons and idBattery as well as with various artists on his own Jewelled Antler record label. Currently, he is editing a book regarding the history and practice of field recording in sound art.

JACK COLLOM was born in Chicago but is a longtime Coloradan. He teaches Ecology Literature and Writing Outreach at Naropa University in Boulder, and works with children abundantly. His *Selected Poems 1955–2000, Red Car Goes By*, was published in 2001 by Tuumba Press, Berkeley.

In the last five years ALBERT FLYNN DESILVER has published over one hundred poems in literary journals all over the country including *Chain, New American Writing, Zyzzyva, Hanging Loose, Conduit, Volt, Slope, Fourteen Hills, Combo, Tinfish, The Hat, Bombay Gin, Van Gogh's Ear* (France), *Poetry Kanto* (Japan). He is editor and publisher of The Owl Press, publishing innovative poetry and poetic collaboration.

BRANDON DOWNING's books include *Lazio* (Blue Books, 2000), *The Shirt Weapon* (Germ Monographs, 2002), and *Cinema & Television Dialogue & Description*, forthcoming in 2004 from Faux Press. He lives in New York City, where he'll always be a kid from California. More work from *Lake Antiquity* can be viewed online at www.fauxpress.com/e/downing.

A longtime resident of New York City, MARCELLA DURAND is the author of *Western Capital Rhapsodies* (Faux Press, 2001) and the current editor of the *Poetry Project Newsletter*. She is also the co-editor of an anthology of contemporary French poetry forthcoming from Talisman House.

JOSHUA EDWARDS co-edits and publishes *The Canary*. His work appears or is forthcoming in *Slate, Hotel Amerika, Skanky Possum, Forklift, Ohio, Smartish Pace*, and elsewhere.

KARI EDWARDS is author of *Iduna* (O Books, 2003), *a day in the life of p.* (subpress collective, 2002), *a diary of lies* (Belladonna 27, Belladonna Books, 2002), *obLiqUE paRt(itON): colLABorationS* (xPress(ed), 2002), and *post/(pink)* (Scarlet Press, 2002). edwards' work can also be found in *Aufgabe, Mirage/Period(ical), VanGogh's Ear, Pom2, Narrativity, Bathhouse*, and *SoMa Literary Review*.

ANDREW FELSINGER is the editor of the on-line 'zine, VeRT, www.litvert.com. His work has appeared in such magazines as *Can We Have Our Ball Back?, Carve, Crack, Mirage Period(ical), Shampoo, Skanky Possum*, and *untitled*. Andrew grew up in the anesthetized suburbs of San Jose. He now makes the decidedly different borough of San Francisco home.

As a child KARL GARTUNG walked (literally) into the spine of a book (the façade of his hometown library in Liberal, Kansas). Somewhat later he helped to found the Woodland Pattern Book Center in Milwaukee, Wisconsin, where he still reads and writes.

KRISTEN HANLON's poems have appeared in *Colorado Review, Crowd, Interim, Volt,* and in the anthology *March Hares: The Best of Fine Madness 1982-2002.* She lives in Oakland and edits XANTIPPE, a poetry journal.

ANTHONY HAWLEY's poems have appeared or are forthcoming in a number of magazines, including *3rd bed, Crowd, Denver Quarterly, Fourteen Hills, The Paris Review,* and *Slope.* He lives in New York City and was educated at Columbia University.

DAVID HARRISON HORTON is author of *Pete Hoffman Days* (Pinball, 2003). His work has recently appeared or is forthcoming in *580 Split, Vert, Tinfish* and *Bird Dog,* among others. He lives and writes in Nanjing, China.

PIERRE JORIS' most recent publications include *Poasis: Selected Poems 1986-1999, A Nomadic Poetics* (essays) and *4x1* (translations of Rilke, Tzara, Duprey & Tengour). He has translated Celan, Blanchot, Jabès, Meddeb, Schwitters and others and has received several PEN awards for translation. With Jerome Rothenberg he edited the *Poems for the Millennium* anthologies. He is professor in the Department of English at SUNY-Albany. In the fall of 2003 he was Berlin Prize Fellow at the American Academy in Berlin.

ANDREW JORON lives in Berkeley, California, where he practices playing the theremin daily. He is the author of several collections of poetry, including *The Removes* (Hard Press, 1999) and, most recently, *Fathom* (Black Square Editions, 2003).

DREW KUNZ divides his time between here and somewhere else. He is currently editor of g o n g chapbooks & co-editor, with Stacy Szymaszek, of the poetry journal *traverse.* Recent poems are in or forthcoming from *Bird Dog, Conundrum, Aufgabe,* and *Oranges & Meat.* His chapbook, *what became of the trip,* was published by Bronze Skull Eight.

BEN LERNER is originally from Topeka, Kansas. His first book, *The Lichtenberg Figures,* is forthcoming from Copper Canyon in the fall of 2004. With the help of a Fulbright Scholarship, he is spending the year in Madrid.

DANA TEEN LOMAX is a poet and educator in the Bay Area. Her chapbook, *Room,* was published by a+bend in San Francisco and her manuscript of the same title won the San Francisco Foundation's Joseph Henry Jackson Award. Poems from her most recent manuscript, *Currency,* are forthcoming in *VeRT,*

Shampoo, Moria, and *sonaweb.* She has received grants from the California Arts Council, Zellerbach Family Fund, and Peninsula Community Foundation. She teaches writing at San Francisco State University and lives with her partner and two-year-old daughter in San Quentin, California.

LISA LUBASCH is the author of *To Tell the Lamp* (forthcoming in 2004, Avec Books), *Vicinities* (2001, Avec), and *How Many More of Them Are You?* (1999, Avec). She is also the translator of Paul Eluard's *A Moral Lesson* (forthcoming in 2004, Green Integer). She is one of the editors of *Double Change*, an online literary journal for French and American poetry.

BRIAN LUCAS was born in 1970. He has a chapbook, *The Head in Spring*, forthcoming in 2004 from Kolormeim Press/Black Square. He lives in Bangkok, Thailand.

SARAH MANGOLD is the author of *Blood Substitutes* (Potes & Poets Press chapbook series) and *Household Mechanics* (New Issues, 2002) which was selected by C.D. Wright for the New Issues Poetry Prize. She is a recent MacDowell fellow and currently lives in Seattle where she publishes *Bird Dog: a journal of innovative writing and art* (www.birddogmagazine.com).

JAMES MEETZE is the author of *Serenades* (Cy Press, 2003) and is one of eleven poets included in *Involuntary Vision: After Akira Kurosawa's Dreams* (Avenue B, 2003). He is the publisher of Tougher Disguises Press and edits, with Dan Fisher, the journal *A Very Small Tiger.* He lives in San Francisco.

Born north of Buffalo, EDRIC MESMER lived and worked between Brooklyn and downtown Manhattan for several years. He currently spends his time in Manchester, England.

CHRISTINE MOORE lives and writes in San Francisco. She recently earned her MFA from the University of San Francisco, and now spends much of her time stitching words together with threads of history.

SETH NEHIL is a sound and visual artist currently living in Brooklyn, NY. Releases include "Sunder, Unite (with Olivia Block)," "Umbra," and "Stria (with jgrzinich)." He is currently collaborating with poet/performer Bethany Wright on the multi-media opera, "Co & Remote." Contact: s_nehil@yahoo.com.

DENISE NEWMAN's collection of poems, *Human Forest*, was published by Apogee Press. Her work has appeared recently in *Fence, Chain*, and *Five Fingers Review* where she is an editor. She teaches at California College of the Arts.

LINDA NORTON is a Senior Editor at the Regional Oral History Office in the Bancroft Library at the University of California, Berkeley. She has published her poems, essays, stories, and collages in a number of little magazines, and has written lyrics for music by composer Eve Beglarian. That piece, *Landscaping for Privacy*, has been performed, translated, and recorded on an Emergency Music CD from CRI. She welcomes new opportunities to collaborate with words, music, and images: lindanorton@earthlink.net.

DENNIS PHILLIPS is the author of nine books of poetry, the most recent being *SAND* (Green Integer, 2002). He also edited and wrote the introduction to *JOYCE ON IBSEN* (Green Integer, 1999). He lives on the landlocked island of Pasadena, where the rivers have the names of their destinations and the ocean is always an hour away.

MONICA REGAN lives and writes in San Francisco, where she grew up. Most of Monica's hours over the past ten years have been dedicated to work in non-profit social change organizations. Poetry reminds her to pay attention to everything else that matters. The work that appears in this issue of 26 is part of a larger project, measured in circles, which emerged from several winter weeks spent in Southwestern New Mexico in 2002, and the road there and back.

STEVE RODEN is a visual and sound artist from Los Angeles. Since 1985, his works have been seen in various international arts spaces including the Hammer Museum, Los Angeles, the MCA San Diego, Gallery E/static, Torino, Italy, the Stadt Gallery, Saarbrucken, Germany, the Centre Pompidou, Paris, the Drawing Center, New York. Since 1993 he has released over 20 cds of his work under his own name as well as the name 'in be tween noise'. The audio work *resonant cities* was released as a cd project on the Trente Oiseaux label in 2002. Upcoming exhibitions include Susanne Vielmetter Gallery, Los Angeles, and a large scale sound installation in collaboration with scientists at Cal-Tech for the Williamson Gallery at Art Center College of Design in Pasadena.

LISA SAMUELS has a new poetry chapbook, *War Holdings*, with Pavement Saw Press. Recent poems and essays appear in *Hotel Amerika, Pom2, Stanzas, New Literary History*, and elsewhere. She teaches at the University of Wisconsin–Milwaukee.

JENNIFER SCAPPETTONE's poetry and prose have recently appeared in journals such as *The Poker, Volt, Xantippe, Can We Have Our Ball Back?, Five Fingers Review, Boston Review*, and *The Poetry Project Newsletter*. Her translations of Amelia Rosselli appear in *Satellite, Mid-American Review*, and *APR*.

ERIC SELLAND's most recent book is *The Condition of Music* from Sink Press. Recent work has appeared in *Untitled* and *First Intensity*. Eric is also a translator of Japanese Modernist and avant-garde poetry. He lives in Belmont just south of San Francisco with his wife Naoko and a wild African hunting dog named Rita.

LAURA SIMS has recently moved to Madison, Wisconsin, where she teaches English Composition at Madison Area Technical College. Her work has appeared or will soon appear in: *Bird Dog, Goodfoot, LIT, Jubilat, Fence*, and *Northwest Review*.

CHRISTOPHER SINDT holds a Ph.D. in English from the University of California, Davis. From 1992-1999, he was the Program Director of the Art of the Wild Writing Conference and since 2000 he has directed the MFA Program in Creative Writing at Saint Mary's College. He has received the James D. Phelan Award and residencies at the Macdowell Colony and the Blue Mountain Center. A chapbook of his poetry, *The Land of Give and Take*, was published in 2002, and he has work forthcoming in *Swerve*.

DALE SMITH edits *Skanky Possum* with Hoa Nguyen. His books *American Rambler* and *Flood and the Garden* are available through Small Press Distribution in Berkeley.

ROD SMITH is the author of *In Memory of My Theories, The Boy Poems, Protective Immediacy, New Mannerist Tricycle* with Lisa Jarnot and Bill Luoma, and *The Good House*. Roof Books published his most recent book *Music or*

Honesty. In translation, the book *Poèmes de l'araignee* was published in France by Bureau sur l'Atlantique in 2003. He edits the journal *Aerial* and publishes Edge Books in Washington, D.C.

KERRI SONNENBERG lives in Chicago where she edits *Conundrum* magazine and co-directs The Discrete Reading Series. She is the author of *The Mudra* (Litmus, 2004) and *Twin Townships Affinity* (Bronze Skull Eights, 2004). Other work has recently appeared in the periodicals *Chase Park, Bird Dog, Antennae, Crayon, Traverse, Pom2,* and *!Factorial*.

Recipient of Stegner, National Endowment for the Arts, and MacDowell Colony fellowships, BRIAN TEARE has published poetry in *VOLT, Boston Review, Ploughshares* and *Colorado Review*, among other journals. His first book, *The Room Where I Was Born*, won the 2003 Brittingham Prize and was published by University of Wisconsin Press. He lives in Oakland, and teaches at California College of the Arts and in Stanford's Continuing Studies Program.

CRAIG MORGAN TEICHER has poems forthcoming in the *Paris Review* and reviews forthcoming in *Chelsea, Electronic Poetry Review* and other magazines.

EDWIN TORRES' (www.brainlingo.com) most recent collaborations include working with the Nurse Kaya String Quartet, The Chamber Dance Project, and the sculptor Nancy Cohen. His publications include *The All-Union Day Of The Shock Worker* (Roof Books), *Fractured Humorous* (Subpress), and the CDs "Holy Kid" (Kill Rock Stars), and most recently "NOVO" (Ooze Bap Records, www.oozebap.org). He is co-editor and designer of the journal, *Rattapallax*, and lives and works in New York City.

LAURA WALKER grew up in rural North Carolina and now lives in Albany, California. Her work has appeared in *Five Fingers Review, syllogism, Fourteen Hills,* and *Bird Dog,* among others. Her book *swarm lure* will be published by Battery Press in the spring of 2004.

MARK WALLACE is the author of a number of books of poetry. This winter, Edge Books published his multigenre collection *Haze*. A book of poems, *Temporary Worker Rides a Subway*, was published recently by Green Integer. His novel *Dead Carnival* is forthcoming from Avec Books. He lives and works in Washington D.C.

ORLANDO WHITE is Diné (Navaho) from Sweetwater, Arizona. His clans are of the Zuñi WaterEdge People, born for the Mexican Clan. He is a creative writing student at the Institute of American Indian Arts in Santa Fe, and will be receiving an Associates of Arts degree in May 2004. He is also a recipient of the 2002 Truman Capote Writing Fellowship and the Naropa 2003 Summer Writing/Poetry Scholarship. His poems have previously appeared in *Red Ink* Magazine and the *Tribal College Journal*.

STEVEN WHITNEY is in private practice as a residential architect in San Francisco.

ELIZABETH WILLIS is the author of three books of poetry. *The Human Abstract* (Penguin, 1995) was selected for the National Poetry Series, and *Turneresque* is just out from Burning Deck. *Second Law*, a booklength poem, was published by Avenue B in 1993. Her poems appear in new issues of *Explosive*, *Open City*, and *Triquarterly*.

JANE WOLFF is a landscape and urban designer based in San Francisco. She has taught at the California College of Arts and Crafts and Ohio State University; since 2002 she has been an assistant professor of architecture at Washington University. These drawings are excerpts from her new book, *Delta Primer*, published by William Stout Publishers. The book and the deck of playing cards that accompany it are available from William Stout Books, San Francisco, California, www.stoutbooks.com.